Kids'
London

GW00417685

**Elizabeth Holt
and Molly Perham**

Kids' London
new edition

illustrations by Jon Miller
maps by Alan Mais

A THOMAS DUNNE BOOK

ST.
MARTIN'S
PRESS

First published 1972 by Abelard-Schuman Ltd. First Piccolo edition published
1978 by Pan Books Ltd and simultaneously by Evans Brothers Ltd. This new,
revised and extended edition first published 1985 by Pan Books Ltd.

Library of Congress Cataloging in Publication Data

Holt, Elizabeth.
  Kids' London.

  "A Thomas Dunne book."
  Summary: An A to X guide to London for young
people listing where to go, what to see and do,
and how to get there. Includes addresses, maps,
and an index.
  1. London (England)—Description—1981—
Guide-books. 2. Children—Travel—England—
London—Guide-books. [1. London (England)—
Description—Guides] I. Perham, Molly. II. Title.
DA679.H64 1987   914.21′04858   86-29653
ISBN 0-312-00403-6

Contents

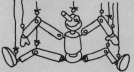

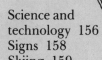

How to use this book

This edition of *Kids' London*, like the previous ones, has been written with the needs of both Londoners and visitors to London in mind, and we hope that it will enable them to look at the city with a fresh eye. By using London Transport's Red Rover and London Explorer tickets, you'll be able to get around very easily at minimum cost and so make the most of London's excellent facilities, many of them free or comparatively cheap.

First-time visitors will, of course, want to see the traditional ceremonies and visit famous buildings, and the sections on **Travelling and Sightseeing Tours**, **Walks**, and **Boats** will probably be of the greatest use to them.

Many Londoners will feel that they know the capital inside out, but we've tried to suggest places off the beaten track for them to visit, and we also hope that some will be encouraged to take up a new interest or get involved in a different sport.

Kids' London is really quite simple to use. Generally speaking, organisations and clubs are given with their addresses and telephone numbers in the sections where they are mentioned. In the few cases where they are not, you'll find them in the index in the back. So are public buildings like museums, together with opening and closing times, and bus and tube directions. We have not included admission charges. As we all know, these change, and anything we put in would soon be out of date. You will see that we have cut out 'The' in the names of most places. The British Museum, for example, has become British Museum, making it much simpler to use the index.

What we do want to emphasise is that if you are making a journey to see something in particular, you really must ring or write (including a stamped self-addressed envelope) or get in touch with one of the organisations under **Information and Information Centres**. You'd be furious if you arrived and found yourself unable to get in, but just like prices, opening and closing times change too.

For the first time, symbols appear beneath many entries:

● refers to the page number where the main entry for a place can be found; all other references are in the index.

🍴 gives a guide to places where you can eat or have a picnic. This doesn't pretend to be comprehensive, but at least you'll know where you can get a snack or a quick cup of tea in many of London's museums.

🆓 means that admission is free. However, in some places, if a special exhibition has been mounted, you do have to pay to see that.

♿ indicates that there is access for wheelchairs, but in some cases this is only partial. Further information will be found in the section called **Handicapped**. You will see that we haven't been able to check on all public buildings, but it's good to know that many of them are in the process of installing or improving facilities for the disabled.

✪ means that you will find it on one of the four maps at the end of the book.

Enjoy yourselves,

EH, MP
February 1985

Calendar
Ceremonial and other events

January

Cutting of the Baddeley Cake:
Robert Baddeley left money in his
will to provide punch and cake for
actors on Twelfth Night

Drury Lane Theatre

Royal Epiphany: gifts of gold,
frankincense and myrrh are made on
behalf of the Queen by Gentlemen
Ushers (6th, 11.30; open to the
public)

**Chapel Royal, St
James's Palace**

**Commemoration of the Execution of
Charles I:** wreath laying at the statue
of Charles I, ceremony at Banqueting
Hall (30th)

**Trafalgar Square,
Banqueting Hall**

Australia Day Service (30th)

St Martin-in-the-Fields

Chinese New Year: celebrations start
in Wardour Street when the eyes of
four exotic dragons are dotted. Lions
and a unicorn lead a lively colourful
procession to dispel evil spirits; red
packets hung outside shops contain
money to entice the beasts and thus
drive away bad luck (about 11.30,
occasionally February)

Soho

Royal Academy Winter Exhibition

Burlington House

International Boat Show
(early in month)

**Earls
Court**

Model Engineer Exhibition
(early in month)

**Wembley Conference
Centre**

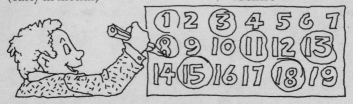

February

Blessing of Throats: people with throat afflictions are blessed at this Roman Catholic church – this takes place every 30 minutes (3rd, 8.00–20.00)

St Ethelreda, Ely Place

Sir John Cass Service: commemoration of the death of the City Sheriff who founded the school named after him in 1709; pupils wear red feather quills in hats and lapels in memory of the blood-stained pen with which he drew up his will as he lay dying (20th, 11.30)

St Boltoph's, Aldgate

Trial of the Pyx: ancient ceremony when the Queen's Remembrancer and a jury from the Royal Mint and the Goldsmiths' Company test the coins of the realm; the verdict is given in May

Goldsmiths' Hall

Scouts and Guides Founder's Day Service (Saturday nearest 22nd)

Westminster Abbey

English Folk Dance and Song Society Festival

Royal Albert Hall

Cruft's Dog Show (early in month)

Earls Court

Stampex

Royal Horticultural Society Halls

National Canoe Exhibition (usually 3rd weekend)

Crystal Palace

Shrove Tuesday (occasionally March)

Pancake Greaze	**Westminster School**
Pancake Race (11.00)	**Lincoln's Inn Fields**
Pancake Race	**Paternoster Square**

March

Bridewell Service: service of dedication and thanksgiving for the foundation of the Bridewell Royal Hospital attended by the Lord Mayor, Sheriffs and pupils from the King Edward VI School, Whitley (2nd Tuesday, 12.00) — **St Bride's**

Oranges and Lemons Service: after a special service, oranges and lemons are distributed to school children; the traditional tune is played on handbells — **St Clement Dane's**

Druid Ceremony: Druid Order celebrates the spring equinox near the site of Tower Hill, an ancient burial ground — **Tower Hill**

Grimaldi Commemoration Service: clowns in full regalia crowd into church for happy service in memory of the most famous clown of all; all clowns are called Joey after Joseph Grimaldi — **Holy Trinity Church, Dalston**

Camden Festival: international music, dance, opera, jazz, choral and contemporary music, exhibitions and other varied activities (last 2 weeks) — **Camden**

East End Festival: theatre, dance, various workshops, exhibitions, children's activities (last 2 weeks)   **Tower Hamlets**

Daily Mail Ideal Home Exhibition (middle of month)   **Earls Court**

London Dinghy Exhibition   **Pickett's Lock Centre**

Oxford and Cambridge Boat Race (occasionally April)   **Putney–Mortlake**

Head of River Races   **Putney–Mortlake**

Easter

St Matthew Passion (Tuesday before Good Friday)   **St Paul's Cathedral**

Presentation of Maundy Money: at one time the monarch washed the feet of the poor, a custom that was discontinued in 1754; now Maundy Money is distributed by the Queen to elderly worthy people – a superb spectacle with magnificent music (London every 4th year, 11.00)   **Westminster Abbey**

Butterworth Charity: a presentation of money and hot cross buns used to be left on tombstones outside the west door of the church for 21 poor widows; now the gifts are for children (Good Friday, following 11.00 service)   **St Bartholomew the Great**

Procession and Carols (Easter Monday)   **Westminster Abbey**

Spital Sermon: Lord Mayor, Aldermen and Common Council walk in splendid procession to the church (2nd Wednesday after Easter, 15.00)   **Guildhall, St Lawrence Jewry**

Easter Parade: marching bands, floats, including floral float from Jersey, music, children's entertainments and other attractions (15.00)

Battersea Park

London Horse Harness Parade (Easter Monday from about 10.00; procession at about 12.00)

Regent's Park

Fairs (usually Saturday, Monday)

Blackheath, Finsbury Park, Hampstead Heath, Hampton Court Green, Richmond Old Deer Park, Wormwood Scrubs

Devizes–Westminster Canoe Race

County Hall steps near Westminster Bridge for finish

Kite Display: enthusiasts meet for their annual extravaganza (Saturday, Sunday)

Blackheath

April

Beating the Bounds of the Tower of London: after a service in the Chapel Royal, a splendid procession walks round the Tower. Choir boys whack each boundary stone with willow wands (every 3rd year, e.g. 1987, 1990, Ascension Day; 11.00)

Tower of London

John Stow Commemoration Service: John Stow was a 16th-century historian. The quill pen in the hand of his statue is removed and replaced by a new one; the Lord Mayor and other dignitaries are present (about 5th, 11.30)

St Andrew Undershaft

Signor Pasquale Favale's Marriage Portion: marriage dowries are presented to 'three poor honest women' aged between 16 and 25 who were born in the City or have lived there for seven years	**Guildhall**
Spring Flower Show	**Royal Horticultural Society Halls**
Westminster Cathedral Spring Flower Festival (end April)	**Westminster Cathedral**
Primrose Day Ceremony: decoration of Benjamin Disraeli's statue (19th)	**Parliament Square**
Shakespeare's Birthday Service (24th)	**Southwark Cathedral**
International Puppet Festival (2 weeks, end April–early May)	**Various venues**

International Model Railway Exhibition (Easter week)	**Wembley Conference Centre**

London Marathon	**Greenwich– Westminster**
Putney and Hammersmith Amateur Regatta	**Putney, Hammersmith**

May

Samuel Pepys Commemoration Service: attended by the Lord Mayor and other dignitaries; music of the period, an address, wreath placed on his memorial (end of month, occasionally June)

St Olave's, Hart Street

London Private Fire Brigades Competition: 66 teams, each with 6 men, compete in a target-spraying competition; bring wellies (occasionally June)

Guildhall Yard

Lillies and Roses Ceremony: commemorating the murder of Henry VI in the Wakefield Tower in 1471. Because the King founded King's College, Cambridge and Eton, representatives join in a procession and lay roses and lilies where he was murdered (21st)

Tower of London

Commonwealth Day: wreaths laid at the Cenotaph (24th)

Cenotaph

American Memorial Day: wreaths laid at the Cenotaph, Lincoln's statue and the grave of the Unknown Warrior (30th)

Cenotaph, Parliament Square, Westminster Abbey

Florence Nightingale Commemoration Service: attended by members of the Florence Nightingale Memorial Committee and Chelsea Pensioners (12th or near)

Westminster Abbey

May Day Rally: march and rally by members of the Labour Party and trade unionists

Hyde Park

Twickenham Week: regattas, concerts, competitive sports, grand carnival procession, fun day, gymkhana (usually mid-May)

Twickenham

Richmond Festival: varied activities, music, drama, exhibitions, dancing (one week towards end of month)

Richmond upon Thames

May Fair: lively day with procession, May Queen, maypole dancing, bands, competitions, music (about 2nd Saturday)

Richmond upon Thames

Canal Cavalcade: Inland Waterways Association's grand parade of decorated craft crossing from one side of Westminster to the other; sideshows, crafts, stalls at Little Venice (usually 2nd Saturday)

London's canals; most going on at Little Venice

London Highland Gathering: bands, pipes, sword dancing, Highland fling, traditional sports, Scottish food, demonstrations (towards middle of month; tel. 556 8916 for information)

Eastway Sports Centre

Chelsea Flower Show (towards end of month; open to public Wednesday–Friday)

Royal Hospital grounds

Royal Academy Summer Exhibition (until mid-August)

Burlington House

Historic Commercial Vehicle Run (1st Sunday)

Battersea Park–Brighton

Football Association Cup Final (2nd or 3rd Saturday)   **Wembley Stadium**

London Canoe Marathon (May Day weekend)   **Thames and canal route; finish at Leaside Young Mariners**

Royal Windsor Horse Show Spring Bank Holiday   **Home Park, Windsor**

Fairs (usually Saturday, Monday)   **Alexandra Palace, Blackheath, Chingford Plain, Finsbury Park, Hampstead Heath, Wanstead Flats, Wormwood Scrubs**

June

Trooping of the Colour: magnificent display of pageantry as Guards troop the colour in front of the Queen; rehearsals held on the two previous Saturdays, first free, second not; apply to the Brigade Major, Household Division, Whitehall SW1 (Saturday nearest 11 June, 11.00)   **Buckingham Palace, Mall, Horse Guards**

Presentation of the Knollys Rose: **Guildhall**
this is in payment of a quit rent imposed by the Lord Mayor in 1381 when the wife of Sir Robert Knollys illegally built a bridge over a road to connect her house with her rose garden (about 24th)

Election of Sheriffs: in a ceremony dating back to 1132, Sheriffs and other officials of the Corporation of London are elected

Guildhall

Oak-apple Day: Founder's Day with Chelsea Pensioners on parade wearing sprigs of oak to commemorate the founding of the hospital by Charles II in 1681 and his escape at Boscobel (usually 1st week in June)

Royal Hospital, Chelsea

Garter Ceremony: service attended by the Queen and Knights of the Order preceded by splendid procession of Household Cavalry and Yeomen of the Guard (Monday afternoon, usually 3rd week in June)

Windsor Castle

Beating the Retreat: impressive military occasion (3 days early in month, 3 days mid-June at either 18.30 or 21.30 when floodlit; tel. 839 6815)

Horse Guards

Festival of the Order of the Knights of St John: members of St John's Ambulance Brigade march to the service

St John's Gate, St Paul's Cathedral

Charles Dickens Commemoration Service: members of the Dickens' Fellowship lay a wreath on the tomb of the author

Westminster Abbey

Early Summer Flower Show

Royal Horticultural Society Halls

Greenwich Festival: theme varies, but includes music, drama, regatta, sports events, talks, walks, workshops, children's events, film festival, Blackheath village fair (usually first 2 weeks)

Greenwich

All England Lawn Tennis Championships: Wimbledon fortnight from 14.00 daily

Wimbledon

Test Match (occasionally July)

Lord's Cricket Ground

Canoe Regatta

Isleworth–Richmond Lock

Twickenham Regatta

Twickenham

Richmond Regatta

Richmond upon Thames

July

Doggett's Coat and Badge Race: sculling race for London's watermen instituted by Thomas Doggett in 1716; he left a legacy for prizes and a splendid red coat and silver badge for the champion oarsman

London Bridge–Cadogan Pier

Swan-Upping: Swan Masters and their assistants, all magnificently dressed, nick Thames swans on their beaks; the number of nicks marks the ownership of the swans

Temple Stairs at Tower Bridge–Henley

Road Sweeping by the Vintners' Company: after the new Master has been installed, the Wine Porter, wearing a clean white smock, sweeps a path clean for the grand procession following him (usually 2nd Thursday)

Vintners' Hall–St James, Garlickhythe

Our Lady of Carmel Procession:
London's local Italian community put
on a colourful procession with dozens
of floats, music and, most
importantly, the statue of Our Lady
(Sunday after 16th, approximately
15.30)

St Peter's, Clerkenwell
Road

City of London Festival: concerts in
St Paul's, Guildhall, Mansion House,
etc., drama, exhibitions, dance

City of London

Lambeth Country Show:
horticultural and flower shows, food
fair, dog show, crafts, local societies,
models, steam engines and many
other activities (usually 3rd weekend)

Brockwell Park

Mall March: splendid performance
by all taking part in the Royal
Tournament (Sunday prior to Royal
Tournament, 10.30)

Mall–Horse Guards

Henry Wood Promenade Concerts
(mid-July–mid-September)

Royal Albert Hall

Royal Tournament: exciting military
spectacular by members of the armed
services and visitors from abroad;
stirring music, precision marching,
exciting displays and competitions

Earls Court

**Metropolitan Police Horse Show
and Tournament:** races,
competitions, police dogs, other
attractions (last Friday, Saturday in
month)

Imber Court,
East
Molesey

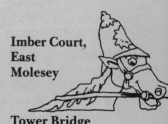

Powerboat Race to Calais and back

Tower Bridge

August

Cart Marking: carts are marked with
the City arms and given a brass
number plate — **Guildhall Yard**

Presentation of a Boar's Head: a
boar's head is presented on a silver
platter to the Lord Mayor by the
Worshipful Company of Butchers;
the ceremony dates back to the
12th century — **Smithfield**

Children's Books of the Year Show — **National Book League**

**European Festival
of Model Railways** — **Central Hall,
Westminster**

Mitcham Fair (mid-August) — **Mitcham Common**

Greenwich Clipper Week
(about 3rd week) — **Greenwich**

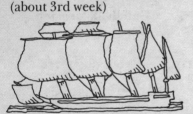

Test Match — **Oval Cricket Ground**

Late Summer Bank Holiday

Greater London Horse Show
(Saturday, Monday, 9.00) — **Clapham Common**

Notting Hill Festival: lively West
Indian carnival with colourful
processions and floats, music and
dancing in the streets — **Portobello Road area**

Fairs (usually Saturday, Monday) — **Alexandra Palace Park,
Blackheath, Chingford
Plain, Hampstead
Heath, Wanstead Flats**

September

Christ's Hospital Boys' March: following a service with the Lord Mayor, Sheriffs and Aldermen present, 300 pupils, headed by the school band, march to the Mansion House for a presentation of gifts by the Lord Mayor

Holy Sepulchre, Holborn, Mansion House

Admission of Sheriffs: splendid procession with Sheriffs-Elect, the Aldermen of their Companies, the Lord Mayor, the City Marshal and other dignitaries to the Guildhall to be presented with their chains of office (28th or previous day if a Sunday, 12.00)

Mansion House, Guildhall

Election of the Lord Mayor: the reigning Lord Mayor and Sheriffs, carrying posies, and the Court of Aldermen choose the new Lord Mayor in a ceremony dating from 1192; City bells ring as the Lord Mayor and the Lord Mayor-Elect leave for the Mansion House (29th, 12.00)

Guildhall, Mansion House

Battle of Britain Day: flypast over London (15th, 11.00–12.00); thanksgiving service (following Sunday, 11.00)

Greater London, Westminster Abbey

British Craft Show (mid-September)

Syon Park

Thamesday (Saturday, mid-September)

South Bank

City of London Flower Show

Royal Exchange

Royal National Rose Society Show	**Royal Horticultural Society Halls**
GLC Orienteering Championship (9.30)	**Lesnes Abbey Wood and Bostall Heath**
British Gymnastics Championships	**Wembley**
London–Brighton Walk (7.00)	**Westminster Bridge– Brighton**

October

Opening of the Law Courts: follows an annual breakfast for Queen's Counsels, a service and a procession through the main hall of the Courts (1st or near)

House of Lords, Westminster Abbey, Law Courts

Quits Rents Ceremony: a billhook and a hatchet are presented to the Queen's Remembrancer by the Controller and the City Solicitor instead of rents for properties; 6 horseshoes and 61 nails are given in payment for the replacement of shoes for the horse which belonged to a knight

Law Courts

Harvest-of-the-Sea Thanksgiving: fish merchants decorate the church with fish and nets, and occasionally a boat (usually 2nd Sunday, 15.00)

St Mary-at-Hill

Lion Sermon: commemorates the escape from a lion by Sir John Gaynor, a Lord Mayor, when he was in Arabia (Monday nearest 16th)

St Katherine Cree

Worshipful Company of Basketmakers' Service: attended by the Prime Warden and his Court

St Margaret Pattens

St Edward's Day Pilgrimage (13th)　　　**Westminster Abbey**

Costermongers' Harvest Festival: pearly kings and queens, dressed in finery, go to a service and make an offering of fruit, flowers and bread (1st Sunday, 15.00)

St Martin-in-the-Fields

Trafalgar Day Ceremony: commemorates the death of Lord Nelson with a naval parade and a service; flags flown read his famous signal that 'England expects that every man will do his duty' (21st)

Trafalgar Square

International Motor Show

Earls Court

Woodworkers' Show (mid-October)

Alexandra Pavilion

Horse of the Year Show (early in month)

Wembley Arena

November

Admission of the Lord Mayor: the outgoing Lord Mayor hands over his insignia to his successor in a dignified ceremony; since no words are spoken apart from the Declaration of Office, this has become known as the Silent Change

Guildhall

Lord Mayor's Show: this custom dates back to 1215 and gave Londoners a chance to see their new Lord Mayor as he went up the Thames by barge to swear allegiance to the monarch at the Law Courts in Westminster; after the Law Courts were moved to the Strand, the Lord Mayor's route has been through the streets of the City (2nd Saturday)

Guildhall, Strand, Law Courts

Remembrance Sunday: the Queen, the Prime Minister, other politicians and representatives of the armed forces lay wreaths at the Cenotaph in memory of those killed in both World Wars (Sunday nearest to 11th, 11.00)

Whitehall

State Opening of Parliament: colourful procession when the Queen, accompanied by the Household Cavalry and Yeomen Warders, drives in the Irish State coach, to open Parliament (early in month)

Buckingham Palace, House of Lords

Guy Fawkes Night: firework displays (5th)

Battersea Park, Burgess Park, Crystal Palace Park

St Cecilia's Day Service and Festival (22nd)

Holy Sepulchre, Holborn

Messiah (Tuesday after Advent Sunday)

St Paul's Cathedral

Veteran Car Run (1st Sunday, 7.30)

Hyde Park Corner– Brighton

Late Autumn Flower Show

Royal Horticultural Society Halls

Caravan Camping Holiday Show (middle of month)

Earls Court

Daily Mail International Ski Show

Earls Court

December

Tower of London Parade: Yeomen Warders are inspected before and after the service (Sunday before Christmas, 11.00)

Tower of London

Christmas Tree in Trafalgar Square: **Trafalgar Square**
lights are switched on; carols around
the tree each evening (from
16.00–22.00)

Midnight Eucharist: candlelit service   **Southwark Cathedral**
(Christmas Eve, 23.30)

Watch-night Service (Christmas Eve,   **St Paul's Cathedral**
11.30)

Watch-night Service (Christmas Eve,   **Westminster Abbey**
11.30)

International Show Jumping   **Olympia**
Championship

Winter Ice Show   **Wembley Arena**

New Year's Eve Celebrations   **Trafalgar Square**

Note: many of the events listed above do not have fixed dates,
and occasionally venues change; for further information ring
the City of London Information Bureau for events in the City,
the London Tourist Board for others.

Daily ceremonies

Ceremony of the Keys

At 21.53 every night the Chief Warder of the Yeomen Warders in the Tower of London lights a candle lantern and makes his way to the Bloody Tower. Here he picks up an escort and goes round locking the West Gate, the Middle Tower and the Byward Tower. He returns to the archway of the Bloody Tower where a sentry shouts, 'Halt! Who goes there?'

'The keys,' answers the Chief Warder.

'Whose keys?' demands the sentry.

'Queen Elizabeth's keys.'

The sentry permits the Chief Warder to pass saying. 'Advance Queen Elizabeth's keys. All's well.'

A little later the Chief Warder whips off his bonnet and cries, 'God preserve Queen Elizabeth!'

'Amen!' shouts the guard and escort, and exactly at 22.00 the bugler sounds the Last Post.

Visitors to this ceremony are restricted, but you can write to the Constable's Office asking for permission to be present.

Changing of the Guard

Buckingham Palace: the new guard accompanied by a band marches either from Chelsea or Wellington barracks arriving at 11.30 to perform a traditional ceremony that takes about 30 minutes.

St James's Palace: the old guard leaves for Buckingham Palace at 11.15, a ceremony that takes very little time to perform.

Note: These ceremonies sometimes only take place every other day in winter.

Horse Guards: there is a 20 minute ceremony on Monday–Saturday at 11.00, and at 10.00 on Sunday. A daily inspection of the guard is made at 16.00.

Recognising uniforms

Chelsea Pensioners

Summer	Scarlet frock-coats
Winter	Dark blue tunics

Guards

Coldstream	Scarlet plumes on right of bearskin; tunic buttons in pairs
Grenadier	White goat-hair plumes on left of bearskin; tunic buttons placed singly
Irish	Pale blue plumes on right of bearskin; tunic buttoms in pairs
Scots	No decoration on bearskin; tunic buttons in threes
Welsh	White plume with green band on left of bearskin; tunic buttons in fives

Household Cavalry

Blues and Royals	Blue tunics; red-plumed helmets
Life Guards	Scarlet tunics, white plumed helmets
King's Troop, Royal Horse Artillery	Blue hussar-type jacket with piped gold braid, red-striped breeches

Royal Bodyguard

Gentlemen-at-Arms	Scarlet tailcoats, gold epaulettes, white gauntlets, gold-striped trousers, Wellington boots, gilt helmets with long swans' feathers; swords and sticks for officers, swords and pole-axes for gentlemen
Yeomen of the Guard	Tudor costume of scarlet trimmed with gold and black, white ruffs, red stockings, red and white rosettes on shoes, flat hat garlanded with Tudor roses, waist belt and cross belt
Yeomen Warders	Identical to Yeomen of the Guard, but without the crossbelt

Action holidays

Do you look forward to the long summer holidays, only to find that after a few days the time begins to drag and you start complaining that there's nothing to do? There's plenty going on in London's parks and museums, if you know where to look.

Museums and centres

Some people think museums are dull and boring, but that's because they simply haven't bothered to find out what they have to offer. Many provide special holiday activities, and these are inventive and varied. Some are half-day or one-day programmes, others are more like clubs with something happening most days of the week. Look in the newspapers or ring up to find out details of the current programme.

Bethnal Green Museum of Childhood has programmes in the summer and Christmas holidays often involving toys and puppets. A recent one was about how toys are made, followed by making your own toy shop.
● See also p.92.

British Museum usually has a holiday event based on some of the exhibits. A recent one was on Roman Britain. There are also talks and trails for children and their parents available from the information desk.
● See also p.56.

Commonwealth Institute has holiday workshops based on Commonwealth customs and lifestyles.
● See also p.88.

Geffrye Museum has projects during the school holidays that offer the chance to get completely involved in topic work. A recent Christmas project called 'Heavenly Scent' included making candles, perfumed paper, toilet preparations, and cooking with spices.
● See also p.160.

Geological Museum organises family events during the holidays both in the museum and around London. You could, for example, go on a geological walk in the City.
● See also p.156.

Horniman Museum has a club for 8–18 year-olds which is open every day except Sundays and Bank Holidays during school holidays.
● See also p.106.

Museum of London organises programmes for families and children during the holidays, based either on the museum's collection or on current exhibitions. These include walks, talks, demonstrations, workshops and films. You can also use the art workshop on your own.
● See also p.40.

National Army Museum has holiday events such as wargaming, plastic modelmaking competitions, and quizzes. You can also take along family war souvenirs and have an expert look at them.
● See also p.42.

National Gallery arranges special activities during holiday periods, including quiz sheets, painting and drawing competitions. A recent quiz involved disappearing cats, young ghosts and a mysterious extra foot in the gallery's paintings.
● See also p.46.

National Maritime Museum runs the Half Deck Club for creative activities which meets on Saturdays and mid-week during the school holidays. This is for members only.
● See also p.55.

National Portrait Gallery has holiday activities for children, and there is a mailing list for those wanting regular information.
● See also p.94.

Natural History Museum has a children's centre in the north hall open on Saturday afternoons and from Tuesday to Saturday in the holidays 10.30–12.30 and 14.00–16.00. Activities include quizzes, trails and worksheets, using microscopes, and sometimes other scientific equipment. This is for those over the age of 10.
● See also p.140.

Science Museum often has special lectures and films. Those in the holidays are designed for the young.
● See also p.157.

Tate Gallery usually has a quiz, trail or competition during Christmas and Easter holidays.
● See also p.47.

Victoria and Albert Museum usually has an event for families at Christmas. Recently members of the London Festival Ballet demonstrated dance steps.
● See also p.139.

Action in the parks

GLC provides free children's entertainment in most GLC parks and open spaces during the summer holidays. As well as puppet shows, Punch and Judy, magic, clowns and street theatre, there's fun with inflatables, a mobile video arts workshop and several Kids' Fun Days. Details of where and when events take place can be obtained from the GLC Parks Department [633 1707], from notice boards in the parks or by telephoning the numbers listed below.

Abbey Wood Park: Finchdale Road, Abbey Wood Estate [310 7494]

Archbishop's Park: by netball court [928 5734]

Avery Hill: café area [850 2666].
● See also p.101.

Battersea Park: adventure playground, Sun Gate [228 2798].
● See also p.146.

Blackheath: Royal Parade Field [858 1692].
● See also p.146.

Burgess Park: Addington Square, north entrance, St George's Way, Wells Way [703 3911].
● See also p.81.

Crystal Palace Park: next to adventure playground [778 7148].
● See also p.146.

Dulwich Park: by children's playground [693 5737].
● See also p.146.

Eltham Park South: near hard tennis courts [850 2031] (swimming pool; refreshments May–September).

Finsbury Park: one o'clock club entrance [263 5001].
● See also p.147.

Geffrye's Garden: children's playground, Cremer Street [985 1957].

Golders Hill: bandstand [455 5183].
● See also p.35.

Hackney Marsh: Daubeney Fields, children's gym area next to Kingsmead Estate [985 8206].

Hainault Forest: near staff yard [500 3106].
● See also p.35.

Holland Park: cricket field [602 2226].
● See also p.147.

Horniman Gardens: bandstand [699 8924].
● See also p.36.

Marble Hill Park: near one o'clock club [892 1900].

Mile End Park: Brickfield Gardens [980 1885].

Oxleas Wood: Crown Woods Lane, grass car park near café [856 1015].
● See also p.146.

Parliament Hill: adventure playground or bandstand [485 4491].
● See also p.147.

Thamesmead: Crossway Park, Hartslock Drive, Northwood Green [310 7494].

Victoria Park: adventure playground [985 1957] (cricket pavilion and Lido; refreshments).

Wormwood Scrubs: Old Oak Common [743 4030].

Information

All London boroughs have local programmes of playschemes and holiday events. Look in your local newspaper, ask at the library, get in touch with the town hall information officer or recreation department, or telephone Children's London or Kidsline (*see* Information and information centres).

Adventure playgrounds

To the casual visitor, adventure playgrounds look like demolition sites crammed with junk. To those who use them, they are marvellous play areas where almost anything might happen. The crazy-looking structures made out of curious and unlikely materials and apparently stuck together with chewing gum are actually carefully built tree-houses, tough assault courses, or tree walks. Besides the free play areas, there are also sometimes games pitches and an indoor area for quieter activities.

Adventure playgrounds are similar to playparks, but they are usually situated outside park boundaries on neighbourhood playsites. They are open after school, during holidays and at weekends. Play leadership staff are always around keeping an eye on what is going on, organising games if they are in demand, and sorting out any problems.

Because they are often on demolition sites or waste ground, adventure playgrounds are closing and opening all the time. This means that any list would soon be out of date. To find out about adventure playgrounds in your neighbourhood, ask at your local library or town hall information desk, or ring one of the organisations listed below.

Organisations

GLC has adventure playgrounds in several of its parks [633 3679]
London Adventure Playground Association, 22 Underwood Road E1 [377 0314]
National Playing Fields Association, 25 Ovington Square SW3 [584 6445]

Aircraft

(*See also* Viewpoints)

Although some people simply think of aircraft as a convenient means of transport, others are fascinated by old planes. After all, when you look at them, it seems incredible that they got off the ground at all. Whichever you are interested in, you'll find that you can see both sorts in London.

Museums

Imperial War Museum has historic aircraft, including some from the First World War, as well as a Mark I Spitfire, a Focke Wolf and a Heinkel from the Second World War, and German V1s and V2s. A display gives you a good idea of how the Dambusters' raid was carried out, and you can see the records of Group Captain Cheshire.
● See also p.42.

RAF Museum, together with the Battle of Britain Museum and Bomber Command Museum, covers all aspects of the RAF from its origins in the Royal Flying Corps. Aircraft, parts of aircraft, equipment, paintings and documents give a comprehensive picture of the development of the RAF. There are usually at least 40 aircraft on show, including an early Sopwith Camel, a Supermarine Spitfire, a Gloster Meteor and a Hawker Typhoon, as well as a man-lifting kite and part of the control car of the airship R33. The galleries reflect life in the service, and it has an RFC workshop and a WRAF hut. The museum has film shows and trails to follow and other exciting things for you to do.

Battle of Britain Museum has aircraft involved in the Battle of Britain on display and a replica of the Operations Room at RAF Uxbridge, as well as numerous items of equipment, documents and other relics. A 20-minute audio-visual show tells you the complete story of this important period.

Bomber Command Museum shows the development of bomber aircraft from the First World War onwards, and has features displaying the life of Bomber Harris and of Sir Barnes Wallace, the man who invented the bouncing bomb used by the Dambusters. (Self-service restaurant; picnic building for booked parties; outdoor picnic area).

🍽 ♿ 🍶 (Not Battle of Britain and Bomber Command Museums).

Museum of Artillery has a display showing how the Thunderbird ground-to-air missile was launched.

Science Museum aeronautics' section has a reproduction of the Wright Brothers' Flyer of 1903, Alcock and Brown's Vickers Vimy in which they crossed the Atlantic in 1919, and the flight deck of an aircraft. There's the Flying Bedstead, Professor Pickard's stratosphere gondola, rockets, and other exciting space exhibits. You can also learn about flying with the aid of a take-off and landing simulator.

● See also p.157.

Event (*see* Calendar)

Battle of Britain Day

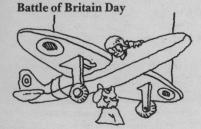

Animals and birds

(*See also* City farms, Conservation, Natural history)

Many of London's parks and open spaces have animal corners, small zoos and sanctuaries. In fact, all over London there are animals in captivity, animals in the wild, animals to ride and animals to feed. If you are more interested in birds, you can see exotic birds and waterfowl or visit bird sanctuaries.

Organisations

Crusade Against All Cruelty to Animals, Humane Education Centre, Avenue Lodge, Bounds Green Road N22, [889 1595] is for those who love animals and worry about their wellbeing. Young Crusaders get a badge, a membership certificate, a magazine, and help and advice about looking after pets and helping hurt animals.

People's Dispensary for Sick Animals, South Street, Dorking, Surrey, [Dorking 888291] has Busy Bees, its junior branch for those aged 5–11. Membership is cheap, you'll get a badge, *Busy Bees News* six times a year, and be encouraged to form hives to raise money for the society.

Royal Society for the Prevention of Cruelty to Animals, Causeway, Horsham, Sussex, [Horsham 64181] has junior members aged 7–17. Members receive a badge, a membership card, and four copies of its magazine a year. There are projects, including puzzles and competitions, and members learn about animals and the best way to look after them.

Young Ornithologists Club, for those under 15 years old, is run by the Royal Society for the Protection of Birds, The Lodge, Sandy, Bedfordshire, [Sandy 80551]. Members receive a badge, a colour magazine six times a year, and the chance to take part in activities including outings and adventure holidays.

Young Zoologists' Club is based at the London and Whipsnade Zoos, and is for those aged 9–18. You get a badge, a membership card, free tickets to the zoo, and queries answered by the information bureau. Older children can become associate members of the Zoological Society of London and attend lectures, brains trusts, forums and film shows. There are also animal collecting trips, field courses and demonstrations in animal photography and other activities.

Animal enclosures, aviaries and sanctuaries

Alexandra Park: animal enclosure.
● See also p.146.

Battersea Park: fallow deer, sheep, waterfowl.

◈ ◉ (Refreshments, March–October.)

Brockwell Park: quail, touracos, toucans, jays and other birds.
● See also p.101.

Clissold Park: crane, fallow and Chinese deer, rabbits, peafowl, mynahs, black-necked swans and other waterfowl.

Dulwich Park: aviary with mots-mots, toucans, budgerigars and other birds; waterfowl on lake.
● See also p.146.

Golders Hill Park: animal enclosure with deer, wallabies, goats, sheep, rabbits, pheasants and other birds; waterfowl on pond and lake.

◉ (Refreshments, March–October.)

Hainault Forest: animals from GLC Mobile Zoos including Welsh mountain ponies, pygmy donkeys, sheep and goats spend the winter in paddocks behind the Fox Burrows.

◉ (Refreshments Easter–October.)

Holland Park: peafowl, geese, crane, pheasants and other birds.
● See also p.148.

Horniman Gardens: wallabies, exotic birds, waterfowl.

⦿ (Tea and snacks, summer school holidays.)

Maryon-Wilson Park: fallow and Chinese deer, Jacob sheep.

Regent's Park: chiff-chaffs, flycatchers, redstarts, willow warblers and other birds best seen in the sanctuary by the lake.
● See also p.149.

St James's Park: Duck Island in the centre of the lake is a breeding ground and sanctuary for pelicans and over 20 species of ducks and geese.
● See also p.149.

Sydenham Wells Park: flamingoes and other birds, small domestic animals.

Waterlow Park: jays, quail, black swans, geese, doves, mynahs and other birds.

Animals and birds in the wild

Blackheath: favourite venue for migratory birds.
● See also p.146.

Epping Forest: foxes, badgers, rabbits, hare and other small animals, many species of birds.
● See also p.147.

Greenwich Park: deer roam freely in the 3-acre wooded park at the East End, also a bird sanctuary.
● See also p.147.

Hainault Forest: deer roaming freely, a variety of other wildlife.
● See also p.35.

Hampstead Heath: foxes, rabbits, squirrels and other small animals, many species of birds.
● See also p.147.

Holland Park: many species of birds in the woodlands on the north side.
● See also p.147.

Lee Valley Park: apart from the resident bird population, many birds use the area as a resting place on their migratory route through Britain; gulls roost at the reservoirs at Chingford while the Rye House Nature Reserve contains an interesting collection of fowl.
● See also p.148.

Richmond Park: hundreds of red and fallow deer, foxes, badgers, weasels and smaller animals.
● See also p.149.

Wimbledon Common and Putney Heath: foxes, weasels and other small animals, many species of birds, waterfowl on lakes.

Zoos

Battersea Park Children's Zoo has some exotic birds and animals as well as more familiar ones. Pygmy goats and sheep wander freely in the enclosures and can be safely handled by children of all ages. On most days you can have a pony ride for a small charge.

● See also p.35.

Chessington Zoo occupies 65 acres of countryside on the outskirts of London and contains hundreds of animals, birds and reptiles, and a children's zoo with friendly animals. There are other attractions such as a summer funfair, a human circus, a boating lake, miniature train rides and Cinema 2001. There are pushchairs for hire for tired toddlers.

Crystal Palace Children's Zoo began as a pets' corner and has grown ever since. Domestic animals wander freely, others are kept in enclosures. There is a penguin pool, and other birds include crane, egrets and rheas. Pony rides are available for a modest charge.

● See also p.146.

London Zoo is in Regent's Park, and it has over 8,000 inhabitants, mainly housed in modern, spacious enclosures. Top favourites include the giant panda, orang-utans, chimpanzees, lions, tigers and elephants. Don't miss the Moonlight World where day and night have been reversed. This means that you can see animals that would only normally be out at night. From Easter to September you can ride a camel, donkey or pony, or take a spin in a llama cart or pony trap. Feeding time is always fun, so watch for

information boards telling you when it all takes place. There's milking in the children's zoo at 15.00 daily. (Refreshments.)

Whipsnade Park Zoo is a conservation centre for many of the world's wildlife and it is also a country home for the animals of the London Zoo. You can drive or walk through the zoo and be transported via the Whipsnade and Umfolozi Railway through huge paddocks to see the animals at close quarters. Dolphin shows are free. The zoo has pushchairs and wheelchairs for hire. (Meals, refreshments.)

Windsor Safari Park has drive-through animal enclosures so that you can view baboons, lions, cheetahs, giraffe, elephants and other animals at close quarters, but on no account get out of your car or lean out of the window. The Killer Whale and the Dolphin Show is always popular, as is the High Dive and a variety of children's amusements. (Meals, refreshments.)

GLC Mobile Zoos visit parks, schools and local shows throughout the summer, concentrating on areas where it's difficult to keep animals. They stay for up to five days and are usually open from about 11.00 to 17.30. Some animals are kept in enclosures. Others, like monkeys, chipmunks, cockatoos and mynahs live in a special caravan, and Shetland and Welsh ponies give rides. Watch noticeboards to see if one's coming your way, or ring the GLC Parks Department.

Other places to visit

Royal Mews *see* Coaches and Carriages.

St John's Barracks permits occasional visits to watch horses being exercised and shod, but these can only be made strictly by appointment with the Adjutant.

Stray and injured animals

Battersea Dogs' Home is a refuge for lost and homeless dogs. About 100 are temporarily housed there, all hoping that either their owners will turn up or that a new one will come on the scene.

Blue Cross Animals' Hospital, 1 Hugh Street SW1, [834 4224] is open 24 hours a day throughout the year for emergency treatment. If you can't afford a vet, ring up, and you and your pet will be directed to the nearest branch.

PDSA has 57 animal treatment centres all over the country, a dozen of them in London. It provides free treatment for those who are hard up. Its London addresses are in the telephone directory.

RSPCA has an emergency service for injured or lost animals, and it provides clinics and hospitals. Find the nearest centre in the telephone directory.

Training of dogs

An untrained dog is a menace. If you are lucky enough to be given a dog, make sure it's properly trained. Ask at the library for the nearest training centre or get in touch with the Canine Defence League, 10 Seymour Street W1, [935 5511]. The RSPCA publishes leaflets on the care of dogs and other animals.

Event (*see* Calendar)

Cruft's Dog Show *see also* Riding.

Archaeology

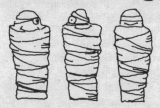

If you are fascinated by the past, then London's the place for you. There are plenty of interesting things to see, some indoors, some out.

Organisations

Council for British Archaeology, 112 Kennington Road SE11, [582 0494] issues a monthly Calendar of Excavations from March to September. This information sheet lets you know of current work being carried out and details of what help is needed. At some sites, unskilled work isn't needed, but at others archaeologists are desperate for it. Do note that you can't join until you are over 16.

London and Middlesex Archaeological Society, c/o The Museum of London, is a lively organisation. Junior membership is amazingly cheap, and once you've joined you'll receive a regular newsletter, be able to attend meetings, and take part in its many activities which include handling material, interesting and amusing lectures, films and trips in and out of London.

Southwark and Lambeth Archaeological Society, c/o Cuming Museum, welcomes young members and offers cut-price membership. It helps in archaeological work when there's an emergency and it's active two or three times a week at various outstations where materials are stored.

Archaeology out of doors

Epping Forest has the remains of two ancient British camps, Loughton Camp and Ambersbury Bank, thought to be about 2000 years old.
● See also p.147.

London Wall Walk, devised by the Museum of London, is the best way of seeing the remains of the Roman and medieval City walls. There are 21 information panels along the line of the City's defences between the museum and the Tower of London. The numbered blue and cream tiled panels start at the surviving remains of the City wall, and reconstructed drawings highlight the City's defences. The route will take you 1–2 hours to complete, and you'll cover about 2 miles of the City streets.

London Stone, thought by some to be the Millarium of Roman London from which distances were measured, is incorporated into the wall of the Bank of China.

Roman Gate Fort, adjoining the Museum of London, is open on the 1st Tuesday in each month 10.30–12.30 and on the 3rd Friday 14.30–16.30.

Temple of Mithras, discovered during excavations in 1954, has had its remains rebuilt in Temple Court, adjacent to Bucklersbury House.

Museums

All Hallows Barking-by-the-Tower is a church dating from AD 675. It has the remains of two Roman floors, a diorama of Roman London, a Roman tombstone, lamps and other exhibits in its crypt museum.

British Museum is a treasure trove with its huge collection divided into sections, including Egyptian, British and Medieval, Greek and Roman, and Romano-British antiquities. The Prehistory Rooms deal with early man, and have relics from the Bronze and Iron Ages.
- See also p.56.

Cuming Museum possesses Roman pottery and the timbers of a Roman ship. Other exhibits give you a good idea of the history of the district.

Guildhall Museum has a collection of antiquities found in the City from Roman times onwards.
- See also p.120.

Museum of London illustrates 2000 years of London's history in marvellously imaginative displays. There's everything from a Roman bikini and a reconstruction of a Roman kitchen to royal relics and treasures. (Coffee shop.)

Museum of the Order of St John offers short conducted tours of St John's Gate and the remains of the medieval priory church.

National Maritime Museum has the Ferriby boats dating from the Bronze Age, the famous Sutton Hoo ship found in the burial mound in Suffolk, and the Graveney boat discovered in the Kent marshes.
- See also p.55.

National Monuments Record is really only for reference or study, but it's useful to know that it contains about a million photographs and measured drawings of the historic architecture of England. There's a separate section of archaeological records and photographs of archaeological sites.

Queen Elizabeth's Hunting Lodge houses the Epping Forest

Museum, with exhibits of local archaeological finds.

Verulamium Museum, in St Albans, has superb Roman mosaics, a relief model of the old Roman city, and a Roman kitchen showing the kind of food Romans ate. You can see jewellery, hair ornaments and tools. Nearby, in the centre of the park, is a hypocaust, and a little further off, the Roman theatre. (Cafés in town; picnic in park.)

Arms and armour

Don't be alarmed if you hear guns booming away in London. Almost certainly it will be the Honourable Artillery Company and the Royal Horse Artillery at work. They fire salutes on special occasions such as the anniversary of the Queen's accession. The Royal Horse Artillery lets off a 41-gun salute, the Honourable Artillery Company a 62-gun salute. The Honourable Artillery Company fires from Tower Wharf, and the extra 21 shots are for the City of London.

The Honourable Artillery Company has its origins in the Trained Bands of the City of London, and it has the right to march through the City with bayonets fixed, drums beating and colours flying. The King's Troop, Royal Horse Artillery, famous for its musical ride, gallops into Hyde Park, gun-carriages dragged behind gleaming horses, and then it fires its salute.

If, however, you're simply interested in arms and armour, there are plenty of places where they're on show.

Places to visit

British Museum has arms and armour from many different civilisations.
● See also p.56.

Bruce Castle Museum illustrates the history of the Middlesex Regiment with drums, flags, weapons and other relics on display.
● See also p.165.

Cabinet War Rooms are 17 feet beneath Whitehall. They are a series of small, austere rooms where Sir Winston Churchill and his war cabinet met, and defence and intelligence staff plotted and monitored the progress of the war. You can see the Prime Minister's combined office and bedroom, and the desk from which he made some of his famous broadcasts. Steel helmets and gas masks hang on pegs, and there are maps pitted with holes where staff put in pins to mark the progress of convoys. In a small room there's the original hot-line, the first telephone with a scrambler, used by Churchill to communicate with President Roosevelt.

Guards' Monument, at the foot of Lower Regent Street, commemorates the 22,000 guardsmen killed in the Crimean War. The figures were cast from captured Russian guns, and the guns piled up at the back of the memorial were actually used at the battle of Sebastopol.

Imperial War Museum has a vast collection of all kinds of weapons and other relics, all illustrating every possible aspect of the two world wars. On the forecourt of the museum you'll be confronted by two enormous 15-inch naval guns. The Development of Modern Warfare is a permanent exhibition covering the period from the American Revolution to 1914. (Refreshments.)

Museum of Artillery in the Rotunda, a tent-like building of 1814 brought from St James's Park when it was no longer needed, contains a large collection of all sorts of ordnance, including crossbows, muskets, rifles, armour and even early rockets. There's a wrought-iron breech loading gun from the *Mary Rose*.

Museum of London has Bronze Age, Roman, Saxon and Viking weapons, pikemen's armour and a splendid suit of armour made in 1630 and worn by the King's Champion in 1761.
● See also p.40.

Museum of the Order of St John has a cannon presented to the Knights of St John in 1522 by Henry VIII.

National Army Museum tells the history of the British army from 1485 to today, Commonwealth armies up to the moment of independence, and of the Indian Army. The Weapons Gallery shows the development of hand-held weapons from medieval times to today's anti-tank weapons. There's masses of things to look at, and lots of things to do, including having a go on the electronic rifle range and finding out how good a marksman you might be. (Cafés in King's Road; picnic in grounds of Royal Hospital.)

Royal Artillery Regimental Museum is full of interesting relics illustrating the history of this famous regiment.

Royal Fusiliers Museum is housed in the Tower of London. There's lots to see, including dioramas of famous battles, uniforms, paintings, weapons, and so on.

Royal Hospital has a battery of guns on the terrace. These were captured during the battle of Waterloo. The museum contains prints, drawings, manuscripts, and other relics.

● See also p.111.

Tower of London is crammed with weapons and armour. In the Sporting Gallery you'll find firearms which were in use between the Middle Ages and 1800. The Oriental Gallery possesses splendidly decorated eastern arms and armour, including armour made to protect an elephant. There's jousting armour, Henry VIII's armour, cannon, lances, helmets and pikes, and there's a massive suit of armour made for a giant of a German. He was 6 feet 10 inches tall.

● See also p.123.

Victoria and Albert Museum possesses fine examples of European and Oriental weapons and armour.
● See also p.44.

Wallace Collection has many fine examples of European weapons and armour, including equestrian armour made for the Count Palatine at the beginning of the 15th century, and a marvellously decorated cannon.
● See also p.48.

Wellington Museum has swords and daggers, including the French sabre carried by the Duke of Wellington at the battle of Waterloo.

Westminster Abbey Museum has the sword, tournament helm and saddle belonging to Henry V.
● See also p.122.

Events (*see* Calendar, Daily ceremonies)

Beating the Retreat

Trooping the Colour

Anniversary of the Queen's Accession

Mall March

Royal Tournament

Art and craft

Painting, printing, embroidery, weaving, woodwork – you can do all these and more at various art and craft centres around London. If pottery, brass rubbing or puppets are your particular interest, there are separate sections for these. Community centres also usually have facilities for art and craft activities: you will find these under a separate heading.

Taking part

Battersea Arts Centre *see* Workshops.

Bethnal Green Museum has an 'open house' workshop in the art room every Saturday. All visitors are welcome. You can do things on your own, but there are a couple of workshop leaders around to suggest activities and lend a hand when necessary. There's also occasional story-telling and painting afternoons for playgroups, but groups must book in advance with the Education Officer.
● See also p.92.

Camden Arts Centre *see* Workshops.

Geffrye Museum has Saturday workshops for painting, printing, music and drama. All children over 7 years are welcome on their own: younger ones must bring a parent.
● See also p.160.

Horniman Museum has a Saturday club open to anyone between the ages of 8 and 18 who can visit the museum fairly often and who enjoys learning about the things in the museum. Activities include drawing, painting, printing, modelling, mask-making, puppet-making, embroidery and pottery.
● See also p.106.

Morley College *see* Workshops.

Museum of London has family workshops on Saturdays, with a variety of art and craft activities.
● See also p.40.

National Maritime Museum *see* Action holidays.

Viewing

British Crafts Centre has changing exhibitions of various crafts, and a shop.

Clerkenwell Green Association of Craftsmen has workshops and exhibitions in the Pennybank Gallery in Pennybank Chambers.

Commonwealth Institute has exhibitions of art and craft from Commonwealth countries.
● See also p.88.

Crafts Advisory Committee Gallery has changing exhibitions of contemporary crafts, an information service and colour slide library of the best of British craftsmen and women.

Crafts' Council Gallery has exhibitions of contemporary crafts, and can give information on all aspects of crafts, including courses. (Coffee bar.)

Glasshouse has a special viewing gallery so that you can watch glassblowing. You are welcome to walk in, but groups should telephone in advance.

Horniman Museum has examples of the art and craft of primitive peoples of the world.
● See also p.106.

Little Holland House in Carshalton was the home of Frank Dickinson, a follower of the arts and crafts movement, artist, designer and craftsman in wood and metal. He built the house to his own design, and it contains hand-made furniture and other craft objects.

Victoria and Albert Museum has a new exhibition of British art and design from 1900 to 1950 with textiles, ceramics, metalwork, furniture, as well as paintings and photographs. Throughout the museum there are examples of art and craft through the ages. The craft shop is a good place to browse and buy presents.
● See also p.139.

Markets

Good places to buy art and craft are

Camden Lock, Jubilee Market and **Piccadilly Market, Greenwich Craft Market** (weekends only) near the *Cutty Sark*.

Art galleries and exhibitions

There are art galleries all over London with magnificent permanent collections which are free. For special exhibitions of a temporary nature there is usually a charge. Exhibitions are often advertised in newspapers, or you can buy the *Art Gallery Guide* to give you up-to-date information.

Bankside Gallery is the home of the Royal Society of Painters in Watercolours and of Painter-Etchers and Engravers. Each society holds a spring and autumn exhibition, and there are others of contemporary and historical work.

Barbican Art Gallery has frequently changing exhibitions, often devoted to London themes, but they have also mounted exhibitions on American folk art, Canadian tapestries and silk screen prints.

● See also p.101.

Commonwealth Institute has a constantly changing exhibition of work by Commonwealth artists.
● See also p.88.

Courtauld Institute Galleries has a collection that covers most periods of art, and is particularly good on the Impressionists. Because the gallery is so short of space it will be moving to a new home in the north block of Somerset House in the Strand.

Dulwich Picture Gallery was London's first art gallery. The superb collection of English and European paintings includes works by Rembrandt, Rubens, Reynolds and Gainsborough.

Guildhall Art Gallery houses the Corporation of London's permanent collection and has loan exhibitions and displays by London art societies.

● See also p.120.

Hampton Court Palace has pictures from the royal collection, including works by Tintoretto, Titian and Correggio. In the Communication Gallery you'll see portraits of women admired by Charles II.
● See also p.145.

Hayward Gallery is part of the South Bank's modern art complex, run by the Arts Council. There are changing loan exhibitions, but they are not cheap to get in. However, there's reduced admission charges after 18.00 Monday–Thursday.

Hogarth's House *see* Famous people.

Holland Park has exhibitions of

art and craft in The Orangery and The Ice House.

● See also p.148.

Horniman Gardens has exhibitions from time to time in The Dutch Barn.

● See also p.101.

Imperial War Museum has an excellent gallery with the work of official war artists such as Stanley Spencer, Paul Nash, John Sargent and Wyndham Lewis.
● See also p.42.

Kenwood House has the Iveagh Bequest with works by Rembrandt, Romney, Reynolds, Vermeer and others. (Refreshments in Old Coach House; picnic in grounds.)

Leighton House is a centre for Victorian studies and holds special exhibitions as well as the permanent collection of paintings by Lord Leighton, Burne-Jones and Watts. Those under 15 must go with an adult

Linley Sambourne House has a collection of works by contemporary artists and cartoonists, including Kate Greenaway.

National Gallery houses the national collection of over 2000 Western European paintings, including at least 800 well-known masterpieces. Don't whizz round

trying to see everything in one go
– you'll become confused and
exhausted. A good way of getting
to know about pictures is to go to
the lunchtime lectures, or the
special holiday activities.
(Refreshments.)

National Maritime Museum has
hundreds of pictures, prints and
engravings of naval subjects.
● See also p.55.

National Portrait Gallery *see*
Famous people.

Queen's Gallery is a small gallery
in Buckingham Palace. There are
portraits of kings and queens and
members of the royal family from
the Middle Ages to the present
day.

Ranger's House houses the
Suffolk collection of Jacobean and
Stuart portraits – noblemen and
their wives all in marvellous
costumes.

Riverside Studios has frequent
exhibitions of art and sculpture,
often very modern.
● See also p.171.

Royal Academy of Arts is best
known for the Summer

Exhibition, which has been held
every year since 1769. To be
exhibited is quite a step forward
for a young artist. There is also a
permanent exhibition of fine
paintings by Reynolds,
Gainsborough, Turner and
others.

● See also Burlington House.

Serpentine Gallery has changing
exhibitions of the work of modern
artists.

Tate Gallery has a large collection
of British paintings of all periods,
modern foreign art and modern
sculpture. It is particularly
famous for its five Turner
galleries. There are special
children's tours during school
holidays, and usually a quiz, trail
or competition at Christmas and
Easter. (Refreshments.)

**Thomas Coram Foundation for
Children** has art treasures from
the Old Foundling Hospital,
including works by Hogarth,
Gainsborough and Reynolds.

Victoria and Albert Museum
houses the National Art Library, a
collection of post-Classical
sculptures, Constables, British
miniatures and watercolours, the
Raphael Cartoon Court and a
massive collection of Oriental art.
● See also p.139.

Wallace Collection is housed in Hertford House, built in 1776. The collection includes pictures by Rembrandt, Watteau and Rubens.

Wellington Museum has a fine collection of Spanish paintings. These were looted by Joseph Bonaparte and were regained by the Duke of Wellington who tried to return them to the Spanish king. The king refused to take 'that which has come into his possession by means that are as just as they are honourable'.

Whitechapel Art Gallery has exciting exhibitions of modern art. (Coffee bar.)

William Morris Gallery was the home of this Victoria poet, artist and craftsman who founded his own business for the manufacture of furniture, wallpaper and church decorations. During school holidays there are special tours, competitions and activities.

Woodlands Art Gallery in Greenwich has frequently changing exhibitions of contemporary art.

Art in the open air

Battersea Park often has exhibitions of sculpture.
● See also p.35.

Bayswater Road has a large selection of paintings for sale on the railings of Hyde Park on Sunday mornings.

Green Park has paintings hanging on the railings along Piccadilly, from Green Park Underground Station to Hyde Park Corner, on Saturdays and Sundays.
● See also p.147.

Hampstead has an annual exhibition in Heath Street organised by the Hampstead Arts Council, at weekends from June to August.

Holland Park has sculpture exhibitions in the summer.
● See also p.148.

The Terrace, Richmond Hill is where Richmond Art Group exhibit their work at weekends from late May to mid-June.

Victoria Embankment Gardens has an exhibition of work for a fortnight in early May.

Astronomy

People have always been interested in what lies beyond earth, and now that space travel has become almost commonplace, even more have become enthusiastic about astronomy.

Clubs and classes

British Astronomical Association, Burlington House, Piccadilly W1, [734 4145] has no age barrier. Members are aged 7–90, and provided you know what astronomy is about, you can become a junior member and pay reduced fees. There are monthly meetings from October–June, and you'll receive a handbook and a journal six times a year. It has sub-sections like the Sun, Moon, Artificial Satellites and Comets, so if you have a special interest, you can learn much more about it.

Junior Astronomical Society, 58 Vaughan Gardens, Ilford, Essex, [518 1708] is also open to those who know the meaning of astronomy. It holds four meetings a year in Holborn Public Library, publishes a quarterly magazine and issues occasional news sheets. You'll find senior members very ready to help and give advice.

Morley College holds family classes on Saturday mornings 10.00–12.00 for those over the age of 8 who are hooked on the idea of time and space. The college suggests fairly simple but absorbing projects for you to work on. Although it has its own observatory, most classes are held at Greenwich Old Observatory.
● See also p.179.

Places to visit

Geological Museum's Story of the Earth gives you a bird's eye view of our planet as seen from space. You'll get a clear idea of the comparative size of each planet and the relationship of one to another. There's also a video on *The Life of a Star*.
● See also p.156.

Greenwich Planetarium is in the Old Royal Observatory and shows projections of the sky and stars. During the term, this is reserved for schools, but during Easter and summer holidays, it's open to those over the age of 7. Telephone for details and times of shows.

London Planetarium has giant Zeiss projectors which transport you across the frontiers of time and space. Admission to the show includes entrance to the

Astronomers' Gallery where special sound and lighting effects highlight the story of great men and science. (Light refreshments; picnic in Regent's Park.)

Science Museum has a display covering the *Planets and Beyond*. You'll be able to examine the Apollo 10 Space Capsule and an Apollo Moon Lander, and see historical instruments including telescopes, heliostats and spectroscopes, orreries, terrestrial and celestial globes.
● See also pp.157.

Athletics

If you are hopeless at running, jumping or hurling things about, you'll know it, but if you feel that you are reasonably good, why not find out just *how* good you might become? Go along to your local club or have a go at a training course. You'll find people very friendly and helpful.

Organisation

Amateur Athletic Association, Francis House, Francis Street SW1, [828 9326] has information about London and Southern Counties athletic clubs.

Athletics tracks

GLC parks with athletic tracks and occasional coaching sessions are at Blackheath, Finsbury Park, Herne Hill Stadium, Parliament Hill, Victoria Park, West London Stadium and Wormwood Scrubs. Telephone [633 1708] for further information.

Some of London's other tracks, some with facilities for field events, are at Belair Sports Ground, Charlton Park, Honor Oak Sports Ground, Hurlingham Park, Mellish Playing Fields, Peckham Rye Park, Southwark Park, St Paul's All Weather Games Area and Vale Farm Sports Centre.

Taking part

Cambridge Harriers meet at Charlton Park track on Tuesdays and Thursdays at 18.00–19.30, and Sundays at 10.30–12.30.

Enfield Harriers meet at the Queen Elizabeth Stadium, Carterhatch Lane, Enfield.

Hammersmith and Fulham's Action Sports has six leaders, all ready to help, whichever sport you're interested in. It offers regular coaching and other activities. Telephone [748 3020 ext. 5124] for further information.

Hillingdon Sports Centre has an annual speed decathalon for those over the age of 14. It consists of 10 varied events ranging from archery to a 600-metre dash.

Hounslow organises a sporting workshop with top level coaching during the summer holidays, and there are sessions for aspiring track and field athletes over the age of 10. Telephone [570 7728, ext. 3222] for further information.

Ive Farm runs introductory athletics courses from time to time for those aged 8–20 and 11–14. Telephone [521 7111] for further information.

Jubilee Hall Recreation Centre has a running club for those who live or work in central London.

Tower Hamlets Athletics Club meets at the East London stadium E3 on Tuesdays and Thursdays at 17.00–19.00.

Victoria Park Harriers has its headquarters at St Augustine's Hall, Cadogan Terrace E9.

Winns Common Trim Trail in Plumstead is a series of exercise stations linked by a quarter of a mile of undulating footpaths. Signs tell you what to do as you reach each station. Telephone [854 9217] for further information.

Events (*see* Calendar)

GLC Orienteering Championships

London Marathon

Boats

(see also Canoeing, rowing and sailing)

For centuries the River Thames was London's main highway. Indeed, London was founded on the banks of the river. At one time it was so crowded with craft that it was said that Londoners could get from one bank to the other without getting their feet wet. They simply scrambled from boat to boat.

Boat trips

The information below applies to the summer months, roughly Easter–September. In the winter there are regular services between Westminster, Tower and Greenwich piers. You should check the times of return sailings at your destination pier. For further information, telephone the London Tourist Board's special river boat information number [730 4812].

Westminster Pier Downstream Services, [930 4097].

Westminster–Tower: (20 minute journey) approximately every 20 minutes 10.20–16/17.00.

Westminster–Greenwich: (45 minute journey) approximately every 20 minutes 10.20–16/17.00.

Westminster Pier Upstream Service, [930 2062].

Westminster–Kew: (90 minute journey) approximately every 30 minutes 10.30–16.00.

Westminster–Richmond: (2½ hour journey) 3 sailings between 10.30 and 12.00 (June–September only).

Westminster–Hampton Court: (3–5 hour journey), 3 sailings between 10.30 and 12.00 (June–September only).

Westminster Evening Cruise: (1¾ hour cruise), 2 sailings at 19.30 and 20.15. Telephone [930 4097] for reservations.

Westminster Circular Cruise: (60 minute cruise) every 30 minutes from 11.30, April–October. Telephone [237 1322] for reservations.

Thames Flood Barrier Cruise: (2½–3 hour cruise) 2 sailings at 10.00 and 13.30. Telephone [740 8263] for further information.
● See also p.157.

Richmond Pier Upstream Service, [940 2244/8505].

Richmond–Hampton Court: every 45 minutes 10.30–18.00.

Richmond Circular Cruise via Teddington Lock: every 45 minutes 10.30–18.00. Telephone [892 0741] for further information.

Tower Pier Downstream Service, [488 0344].

Tower–Greenwich: (35 minute journey) every 20–30 minutes 11.30–17.00.

Tower Pier Upstream Service, [488 0344].

Tower–Westminster: (20 minute journey) every 20–30 minutes 11.20–17.00.

Tower Pier Ferry Service to HMS *Belfast*, [407 6436], 20 minute frequenty 11.00–18.00 when HMS *Belfast* is open.
● See also p.54.

Tower Pier Audio-Visual History Cruise: (2 hour lunchtime cruise, 2½ hour dinner cruise). Telephone [488 0344] for further information.

Charing Cross Pier Downstream Service, [231 1744].

Charing Cross–Tower or Greenwich: approximately every 30 minutes 10.30–16.30.

Charing Cross Evening Cruise: every evening at 19.30. Telephone [930 0971] for further information.

Other boat trips

Pride of Lee is a super waterbus cruising along lovely stretches of the River Lee from the Boat Centre, Broxbourne. There are sailings on Sundays in the summer and at most weekends during the summer holidays (afternoons only). Rowing boats and motor boats can also be hired. Telephone [Hoddesdon 462085] for further information.

Thames Mini Cruises are a combined rail/river trip. You leave Paddington by train, have a trip along the Thames, and return by train. Contact Central Enquiry Bureau, [723 7000] at Paddington Station, Paddington W2 1HA, main BR stations, or try local travel agents.

Tidal Cruisers specialise in lunchtime and evening excursions Wednesday–Friday at 12.30 and 20.00. At lunch time, lunch baskets or sit-down meals are available; in the evening, supper baskets only.

Woolwich Free Ferry, although not quite in the same class, really is for free.

Canal trips

Colne Valley Passengerboat Service operates trips from Uxbridge Lock along the Grand Union Canal main line May–September.

Eastern City Canal Ferries run trips from Limehouse Basin to Camden Lock and back.

Jason's Trip lasts 1½–2 hours as you cruise through Regent's Park to Camden Lock and back. The timetable varies, but it usually operates Easter–October. Ring for details.

Jenny Wren takes you on a 1-hour jaunt from Camden Lock to Little Venice, Easter–September. Telephone [485 4433] for details.

Porta Bella Packet has a 2-hour cruise through Paddington to Little Venice, past the London Zoo to Cumberland Basin and back, but if the trip's too long, you get off at intermediate points. It operates Easter–September at

14.00–16.00 with more frequent trips in summer. Telephone [960 5456] for information.

Zoo Waterbus is the nicest way of visiting the London Zoo. The trip takes about 30 minutes, and it's in April–September from 10.00–16.45. The fare includes reduced admission to the zoo.

● See also p.37.

Boats for hire

You can hire boats at Alexandra Palace Park, Battersea Park, Burgess Park, Crystal Palace Park, Dulwich Park, Finsbury Park, Regent's Park, the Serpentine in Hyde Park, Victoria Park, Ruislip Lido and Thamesmead. If you're thinking of going at weekends or during the holidays, get there early before the queues build up.

Hammertons, near Orleans Gardens in Twickenham [893 9620], has rowing boats for hire Saturday–Thursday from 10.30–18.00, and Fridays 14.00–18.00.

Lee Valley Park has sailing on the King Geoge V and Banbury reservoirs.
● See also p.148.

Thames Skiff Hire, on the towpath near Richmond Bridge [940 6868], has rowing boats for hire daily 9.00–18.00. Note that the young must be accompanied by an adult.

Boats to visit

HMS *Belfast,* the biggest and the most powerful cruiser ever built for the Royal Navy, is moored opposite the Tower of London. There are seven decks to explore, punishment cells to examine, and you can visit the engine room, the boiles and the bridge, see films and looks at records detailing her history. (Refreshments.)

● See also p.53.

Cutty Sark, built as a tea clipper in 1869, is permanently moored at Greenwich, and she's a dazzling sight. You can explore her and see the Long John Silver collection of figureheads down below. The young must be accompanied by an adult. (Cutty Sark Gardens: refreshments.)

Gipsy Moth IV, moored alongside the *Cutty Sark*, is the famous ketch in which Sir Francis Chichester sailed single-handed around the world in 1966–7. (*See Cutty Sark* above.)

Historic Ships Collection is moored at St Katherine's Dock. It's a busy and colourful place to visit with its two basins. One has moorings for private craft, and the other contains the collection of seven historic ships, including the RSS *Discovery*, the Nore lightship, a three-master topsail schooner and a steam coaster. They can all be visited, and there are exhibitions on board. (Refreshments.)

Museums

National Maritime Museum stands on the site of the Tudor royal palace of Placentia, where Elizabeth I was born. The museum is crammed with exhibits, and so many of them are *so* splendid that it's difficult to single things out. You can see the development of wooden and steamships, and follow the history of astronomy and navigation. There are pictures, uniforms, dioramas, modern naval items, a collection of figureheads, relics of Lord Nelson, and a museum of yachting. Whatever else you do, don't fail to visit the Barge House. It really is impressive.

If you are fortunate enough to live in Greenwich, Lewisham or Tower Hamlets, you can buy a really cheap neighbourhood ticket by producing some form of identification at the museum information desk. If you go several times a year, this really is a money saver. (Restaurant, picnic in grounds. Partly accessible.)

Science Museum has well over 2000 items showing how man conquered the sea from earliest times, and it illustrates the development of navigation. There are sailing ships and small craft, a section on steamships of war, marine engineering, and models of 18th-, 19th- and 20th-century docks and dockside equipment.
● See also p.157.

Events (*see* Canoeing, rowing and sailing)

Books

There are bookshops all over London, but the centre of the book trade is Charing Cross Road, where there are lots of bookshops selling both new and secondhand books.

You should make use of your local libraries. Most are very good, and some are marvellous, particularly in the holidays, when they buzz with activity.

Organisations

Federation of Children's Book Groups, Aptonfields, Houndslow Green, Barston, Nr Dunmow, Essex, [0731 820024] is intended to further the interest of both parents and children in reading. Branches organise meetings, occasional sessions with authors talking about their work, sales of secondhand books, and so on.

Library Association, 7 Ridgmount Street WC1, [636 7543] has information about all London libraries.

National Book League, 45 East Hill SW18, [870 9055] has a permanent reference library of children's books published in the previous 2 years, and a separate collection of children's poetry. In late July or August it holds an annual exhibition of the best children's books published in the previous 12 months.

National Children's Book Week takes place every year early in October. Special events are organised by librarians, and there are often fairs at which you can meet authors and artists, and take part in lots of activities and competitions.

Museums

Bishopsgate Institute has a marvellous collection of over 5000 books on London, as well as prints and water-colours.

British Museum is a treasure trove for book lovers. There's a permanent exhibition of books and manuscripts, a superb collection of printed books and manuscripts, the Manuscript Saloon, where you can see the beautiful *Lindisfarne Gospels* and musical manuscripts, and the King's Library, notable for superb Oriental manuscripts, and early books, including the first printed edition of Chaucer of 1478 and the first printed English Bible of 1535, as well as Shakespeare's first folio. (Picnic in forecourt, nearby squares.)

Dickens' House has pages of original manuscripts by Charles Dickens, hundreds of letters, and first editions.
● See also p.94.

Guildhall Library was founded in 1425 and has well over 140,000 volumes on London, and hundreds of manuscripts and prints.
● See also p.120.

Keats' House has letters and manuscripts belonging to the poet.

Museum of London has books and documents about London, and some lovely illuminated manuscripts.
● See also p.40.

Museum of the Order of St John has the beautiful Rhodes Missal, 16th-century books and other documents.

Public Record Office contains the national archives from the Norman Conquest to today. There's the Domesday Book, Shakespeare's will, letters warning of the gunpowder plot, Wellington's dispatch from Waterloo, the autographs of kings and queens, and other fascinating exhibits.

Royal Hospital has manuscripts and prints relating to the hospital and its pensioners.
● See also p.111.

St Bride's Crypt Museum has pages from old newspapers, maps and documents, a Breeches Bible of 1560 and other exhibits.

Science Museum has early printing presses, monotype and linotype, photo-composing machines, writing implements of all kinds, and typewriters. There's a display illustrating the history of newspapers and the development of paper-making.
● See also p.157.

Books in markets

Farringdon Road Market has half a dozen book stalls, all run by the same man. Other markets with occasional stalls are at Camden Lock, Camden Passage, Portobello Road and Westmoreland Road.

Piccadilly Book Fair, open Wednesday–Friday in the summer only, is located between the Royal Academy and Burlington Arcade. It has a good selection of children's annuals, but they aren't cheap.

Bookshops

It's quite impossible to list every good bookshop catering for children in London. Most of them are very welcoming, and many put on special events for the young. It's always worth dropping into the larger branches of John Menzies and W. H. Smith to see

what's new in the paperback world.

Angel Bookshop, 102 Islington High Street N1, [226 2904].

At the Sign of the Dragon, 131 Sheen Lane SW14, [876 3855].

Bookboat, Cutty Sark Gardens, Greenwich SE10, [853 4383].

Bookspread, 58 Tooting Bec Road SW17,]767 6377].

Children's Bookshop, 29 Fortis Green Road N10, [444 5500].

Children's World, 229 Kensington High Street W8, [937 6314].

Crouch End Bookshop, 60 Crouch End Hill N8, [348 8966].

Fanfare Bookcentre, 2 Chingford Road E17, [527 4296].

Foyle's, 119–125 Charing Cross Road WC2, [437 5660].

Hammick's, 1 The Market, Covent Garden WC2, [379 6465].

Hatchards, 187 Piccadilly W1, [439 9921].

High Hill Bookshop, 6 Hampstead High Street NW3, [435 2218].

Harrods, Brompton Road SW1, [730 1234].
● See also pp.000.

Islington Books, 268 Upper Street N1, [226 3475].

Liberty and Co., Regent Street W1, [734 1234].
● See also p.75.

Muswell Hill Bookshop, 72 Fortis Green Road N10, [444 7588].

Owl Bookshop, 211 Kentish Town Road NW5, [485 7793].

Pan Bookshop, 158 Fulham Road SW10, [373 4997].

Penguin Bookshop, Unit 10, The Market, Covent Garden WC2, [379 7650].

Reading Matters, Lymington Avenue, Wood Green N22, [881 3187].

Riverside Studios, Crisp Road W6, [748 3354].
● See also p.171.

Selfridges, 400 Oxford Street W1, [629 1234].

Swiss Cottage Books, 4 Canfield Gardens NW6 [586 1692].

Brass rubbing

Few churches now allow people to rub their original brasses since they have found that constant rubbing erases some of the details. Fortunately there are several places where keen brass rubbers can go and rub replicas of famous brasses.

All Hallows Barking-by-the-Tower is one branch of the London Brass Rubbing Centre. There are replicas to rub, and you can also look at some of the best original brasses in London.
• See also p.40.

St James's Church, Piccadilly, is the other branch of the London Brass Rubbing Centre. It contains a unique collection of facsimile old English church brasses. Brass rubbing materials are provided and are also on sale. Choose from medieval knights and ladies, kings, merchants, judges, scholars, children and animals. Admission is free, but a charge is made for the use of brasses and materials.

Westminster Abbey has replicas of kings, queens, lords and ladies from the Abbey's history and from all over England.
• See also p.122.

Bridges and tunnels

We zoom from one side of the Thames to the other without a second thought, but for centuries crossing the river was a bit of a problem. Up to 1739, there was only one bridge – London Bridge. London expanded as people flocked to the capital to live and work, and so the crush of people trampling over the bridge became greater and greater, and the horse-drawn traffic became snarled up. So, gradually new bridges were built in spite of the loud protests of the watermen, who ferried people from bank to bank.

Albert Bridge is a cantilever and suspension bridge, built in 1873, and named after Prince Albert. Nearby is the figure of Atlanta.

Barnes Railway Bridge, opened in 1849, is constructed of iron.

Battersea Bridge, which is really rather ugly, was opened in 1890. Many regretted the destruction of the old wooden bridge, often painted by Whistler.

Battersea Railway Bridge was built to connect the north of England to the south.

Blackfriars Bridge, built in 1899, was named after a priory of black-robed Dominican Friars which backed onto the Thames. The hull of a Roman boat was discovered nearby.

Blackwall Tunnel was an engineering triumph when it was completed in 1897 after 8 years work. A twin tunnel was opened in 1967.

Cannon Street Railway Bridge was built by the South Eastern Railway Company in 1886. A train shed sticks out on one side, adding to the general air of depression.

Chelsea Bridge is a suspension bridge, which replaced an older bridge in 1934.

Chiswick Bridge, opened in 1933, has a concrete arch 150 feet long, making it the longest span of all the bridges.

Dartford Toll Tunnel wasn't constructed until 1967, but it had been planned as long ago as the 1820s. It connects Dartford and Purfleet, and is for vehicles only.

Fulham Railway Bridge, built in 1889, is a trellis girder bridge, and has underground trains rolling across it in the open air. Running alongside is a footbridge.

Greenwich Foot Tunnel connects Greenwich with the Isle of Dogs. On the Greenwich side, the entrance to it in Cutty Sark Gardens is concealed by a dome with a cupola. The other end of the tunnel is in Island Gardens.

Hammersmith Bridge is a decorative suspension bridge, built in 1887, and it incorporates part of an earlier bridge. From it, you can get a view of the small group of 18th-century houses in Hammersmith Mall.

Hungerford Bridge is a separate footway running alongside Charing Cross Railway Bridge.

Kew Bridge's official name is the King Edward VII Bridge, named after the monarch when he opened it in 1903.

Kew Railway Bridge is a quite nice lattice girder bridge of 1869.

London Bridge, the nursery rhyme one, was started in 1176, and not finished until 1209. The rents from the shops, houses and the Chapel of St Thomas à Becket helped to pay for its upkeep. This was one of the places where the heads of executed traitors were stuck on spikes, just to remind Londoners that it paid to be loyal. A huge waterwheel was constructed alongside the bridge, and for many years it pumped water for London's inhabitants.

In 1831, the old bridge was pulled down, and a five-arched granite bridge replaced it, but as time went on, it proved to be too narrow to cope with increased traffic. So, it too was demolished, and a new one opened in 1973, while the old bridge was transported across the Atlantic to a new home in the USA.

Putney Bridge was built in 1886, and widened in 1933.

Richmond Bridge is a graceful five-arched bridge, which replaced a toll bridge of 1777.

Richmond Footbridge, built in 1894, has three weir gates beneath the arches, which when lowered, form a lock.

Richmond Railway Bridge, constructed of iron and concrete, was opened in 1848.

Rotherhithe Tunnel was built between 1904 and 1908. Alongside it are the remains of an earlier tunnel which collapsed when it was almost completed.

Southwark Bridge, opened in 1921, took 8 years to complete, and replaced a 19th-century structure.

Thames Tunnel, officially the Wapping–Rotherhithe Tunnel, was constructed by Sir Marc Isambard Brunel. It took 11 years to complete, and the job was twice abandoned when it was flooded by the Thames. In 1827, to show that he still had faith in the project, Brunel gave a banquet inside it.

At last, in 1843, it was opened. Although built as a road tunnel, it's now used by London Transport.

Tower Bridge, built in 1894, is unmistakable with its Gothic towers and high lattice walkway. When ships approach, they fly a ball and pennant or show two red vertical lights at night. At the same time they give a long and three short blasts on their sirens, and then the traffic lights at either end of the bridge turn red and a warning bell rings, and slowly the bascules are raised so that ships can pass beneath it.

Tower Subway was built to transport passengers to Bermondsey. There was a 60-foot shaft, and stationary engines pulled the carriages along, rather like a cable car. Nowadays, the tunnel is used to carry service pipes.

Twickenham Bridge is a wide, pleasant, concrete bridge, opened in 1933.

Vauxhall Bridge, hardly London's most beautiful bridge, was completed in 1906, replacing an earlier iron bridge.

Victoria Railway Bridge is 900 feet long. At 132 feet wide, it was the broadest in the world at the time it was opened in 1895.

Waterloo Bridge was completed in 1937, but not officially opened until 1945. It's considered to be the most graceful of all London's bridges, and from it you get a stunning view both upstream and downstream.

Woolwich Tunnel, connecting North Woolwich and Woolwich, was opened in 1912. It was only built because people complained about the constant interruptions and delays on the Woolwich Free Ferry service.

Camping

Whether you are a Londoner trying to get out of London or a visitor trying to get in, if you are hoping to camp, you should get as much advice as possible. Your holiday could be completely ruined if you left everything to chance.

Organisation

Camping and Caravaning Club Ltd, 11 Lower Grosvenor Place SW1, [828 1012] has a flourishing youth section for those aged 12–18. You'll learn how to be an efficient camper and once you've passed the test, you'll have full club status and be allowed to use its excellent camping sites. Members receive a handbook, a bi-monthly intermediate booklet, technical advice and information on camping sites both at home and abroad.

Camping sites in London

Abbey Wood Cooperative Woods Camping and Caravan Site, Federation Road SE2, [310 2233] is open throughout the year and has showers, a laundry, gas available, and a shop.

Crystal Palace Caravan Harbour, Crystal Palace Parade SE19, [778 7155] is a well-equipped site open throughout the year.

Eastway Camp Site, Temple Mills Lane E15, [534 6085] is an 80-pitch site in 40 acres of parkland and only 4 miles from central London. You'll have the use of sports facilities and the cycle circuit at the nearby Eastway Sports Centre.

Grange Farm Leisure Centre, High Road, Chigwell, Essex, [500 0121] is open June–August for large-size tents only.

Hackney Marsh International Camping, Millfields Road E5, [985 7656] caters for both campers and motorised caravans but is open only June–August.

Pickett's Lock Centre, Pickett's Lock Lane N9, [803 4756] is a good 6-acre site not too far from central London. Its facilities include a bar, a cafeteria, a crèche, and leisure and sports opportunities, but it's open only in the summer.

Sewardstone Caravan Park, Sewardstone Road, Chingford E4, [529 5689] caters for both campers and caravaners. Its facilities include modern toilet blocks, a shop and a launderette.

Canoeing, rowing and sailing

More and more people, it seems, want to 'mess about in boats', but messing about isn't good enough these days. If you want to enjoy yourself on the water, then you must make sure that you're not going to be a danger to yourself or anyone else. You should join a club or go on a course so that you learn how to handle craft properly.

Organisations

Amateur Rowing Association, 6 Lower Mall W6, [748 3632] is the governing body of this sport. It publishes an annual almanack which lists details of clubs and events. The age at which junior members are admitted depends on individual clubs, but it's not advisable to embark on rowing until you are at least 10 years old.

British Canoe Union, 45 High Street, Addlestone, Weybridge, Surrey, [Weybridge 41341] is the governing body of this sport. It gives advice, organises competitions, runs a coaching scheme and an advisory service, and offers cheap cadet membership for the first year. It publishes a comprehensive canoeing handbook, a guide to available waterways, and has leaflets on all aspects of the sport.

Royal Yachting Association, Victoria Way, Woking, Surrey GU21 1EQ, [Woking 5022] controls this sport. It's ready to provide advice, and it has details of all recognised teaching establishments.

Sea Cadets Association, Broadway House, The Broadway SW19, [540 8222] will be able to tell you which of its 400 branches is near you. Boys and girls learn all seafaring skills, including sailing, canoeing at evening and weekend sessions. There's usually a week's training in offshore activities during the year.

Clubs and centres

Banbury Sailing Centre offers board and dinghy sailing courses to RYA standards at all levels.

Beauchamp Lodge is a youth club that's alive with activity. There's canoeing and sailing, but you must be able to swim. It accepts people from the age of 7 as long as they are accompanied by an adult. The club also owns the *Erica*, a traditional narrowboat which is available for day trips or residential cruising. The club is open Monday–Friday evenings and during the school holidays, but it's very popular, so if you want to do something in particular, ring up and make sure that there's room for you.

George Green's Canoeing and Sailing Club runs courses at the George Green Centre.
● See also p.162.

Greenwich Yacht Club operates from the Tideway Sailing Centre. Ring for details of courses.

Hammersmith and Fulham Canoe Club is a friendly and active organisation. For details of membership, go along to one of its pools sessions on Fridays at 16.00–17.00 and Saturdays at 9.00–10.00, or telephone [748 3020, ext. 293].

Islington Boat Club is primarily for local residents. The club house is a boat moored in the City Basin of Regent's Canal. Membership is open to those aged 9–16 who can swim approximately 45 metres. It's open at weekends and throughout the summer holidays.

Jubilee Waterside Centre is for those over the age of 11 who can swim at least 23 metres wearing light clothing. It offers canoeing at all levels, and there are star tests, wild water slalom and marathon competitions.

Leaside Youth Centre is a marvellous place. It's open every evening and throughout the summer holidays, but it is closed for 2 weeks at Christmas. It has about 150 canoes and other craft, and facilities for building canoes. There's a club house, film shows, and weight training. There are 2 pools so that you can learn capsize drill and advanced canoeing, but you've got to be over 12 to join, and you must be able to swim.

Michael Sobell Sports Centre runs Sobell Outdoors, using both kayaks and canoes. There are pool sessions and an imaginative series of events throughout the year such as a canoe/kayak tour of London.
● See also p.163.

National Maritime Museum's Half-Deck Club has a boat-building shop where you can learn to make traditional craft up to 12 feet long.
● See also p.55.

North London Rescue Commando has a full programme of canoeing, rowing, life-saving, rescue drill and climbing, and it operates a rescue service for events like regattas, some in London, some on the coast. You must be able to swim at least 50 metres before you can join. The club meets Tuesday–Thursday 18.30–21.30, and in daylight hours on Saturdays.

Pirate Club offers young people in Camden instruction in recreational water activities. It's based in a castle, and has a large fleet of craft of all kinds, including a 12-berth narrowboat.

Shadwell Basin Project is a good water recreation centre, and offers canoeing, sailing and windsurfing.

South East London Aquatic Centre runs courses in canoe training. Check for the minimum age to take part. Generally, the centre's open Tuesday–Sunday throughout the year, but closing times vary.
● See also p.100.

Southmere Education Boating Centre is open Monday–Friday, on occasional Saturday mornings, and during the first 4 weeks of the summer holidays 10.00–15.00. So, if you're over the age of 12, and can swim at least 45 metres, this is the place for you.

Surrey Docks Sailing School is primarily for Southwark youth aged 10–20, who can swim at least 90 metres in light clothing. It's open for canoeing, sculling and sailing most evenings from 17.00–21.00, and occasionally on Saturday and Sunday 9.00–17.00.

Tonbridge School Clubs Ltd has canoeing for juniors and teenagers at weekends.

Trafalgar Rowing Centre runs rowing courses for beginners, intermediate and advanced rowers, and organises events such as the Trafalgar Regatta. Ring to find out the age at which you can join [858 9568].

Welsh Harp Sailing Base is for those aged 14–20 who are members of recognised youth organisations. It's open at weekends, on summer evenings, and throughout the summer holidays.

Events (See Calendar)

International Boat Show

Oxford and Cambridge Boat Race

Head of the River Races

London Dinghy Exhibition

Putney and Hammersmith Amateur Regatta

Canoe Regatta

Twickenham Regatta

Richmond Regatta

Doggett's Coat and Badge Race

Powerboat Race to Calais

Thamesday

Devizes–Westminster Canoe Race

London Canoe Marathon

Canal Cavalcade

Cars, cabs and commercial vehicles

Whenever old vehicles are on parade, they're always surrounded by people of all ages, gazing at them with admiration.

Organisation

Veteran Car Club of Great Britain, Jessamine House, 15 High Street, Ashwell, Hertfordshire, [Ashwell 2818] welcomes enthusiasts of all ages. Junior members receive a badge and six gazettes a year saying what's going on where.

Museums

Imperial War Museum has vehicles of all kinds, including Old Bill, a London bus used to carry troops to the front line during the First World War.

● See also p.42.

London Transport Museum is in the middle of historic Covent Garden. Here you'll see the whole spectrum of London's public transport – gleaming buses, trolley buses, trams and trains, models and maps, posters, photographs and audio-visual displays. There's lots to do. Press a button, and an early underground lift starts to move; have a go as a signalman, and find out how a dead man's handle works on an underground train. There are films and activities every weekend, and special exhibitions are mounted from time to time. (Coffee shop.)

Museum of London has quite a number of exhibits, including a 1936 Ford, one of the first production models made in this country.

● See also p.40.

Science Museum has splendid motor cars, including an 1888 Benz, the oldest motor car still in running order, the earliest Rolls Royce of 1904, the world's first gas-turbine car, and other

exhibits. You can also see section chassis, engines and accessories which show how road vehicles work.

● See also p.157.

Syon Park is the home of the British Motor Industry Heritage Trust, which has lots of vehicles. There are 3 and 4-wheel Wolesleys, steam cars, Jaguars, MGs, Rovers, an 1896 Thorneycroft Steam Wagon, a 1901 Goodwin and Barsby Single Toggle Jawcrusher, a prototype electric car, and many others, all in sparkling condition. Ring for news of special events. [580 0881]. (Cafeteria.)

Events (*see* Calendar)

Historic Commercial Vehicle Run

Veteran Car Run

International Motor Show

Chess

Chess players, it seems, get younger and younger these days, and more and more clubs are throwing their doors open to junior members. We've listed some of them, but if there isn't one in your locality, why not go along to your library and find out if there's one nearby? You'll probably find that you are welcome.

Competitions

City Chess Novice Championship is the ideal tournament for newcomers to competitive chess. For further information, contact Mr G. Goodwin, Highbury Fields School, Highbury School N5.

Junior Chess Congresses are organised each year, attracting competitors from all over the country.

Richmond upon Thames has a junior chess tournament during its Festival Week.

Clubs and centres

Canada Villa Youth Centre, Pursley Road NW7, [959 2811] is where 100 young chess players meet during term-time on Tuesdays 17.00–20.00, and where coaches are ready to help them to improve their game. Learn the basic moves, and go along and join them. Ring Tony Corse, [775 9080] for further information.

Hampstead Chess Club meets at Hampstead Baptist Church Hall, Heath Street NW3 every Monday

19.00–22.30. Those who already know how to play and are over the age of 14 are welcome.

London Central YMCA runs a junior club on Sundays 16.00–18.30. You should know the moves before you join, but if you don't, call in and get some help. As soon as you're competent, you'll be able to play with seniors on Mondays 18.30–20.15.

● See also p.179.

Mates Chess Club is really thriving. It meets at Harrow Leisure Centre on Mondays (excluding Bank Holiday Mondays) 17.30–19.30. The youngest members are from 5 upwards, and although all are welcome, it runs more smoothly if new recruits understand the basic moves.

Muswell Hill Chess Club, which has recently started a junior club, meets at Tetherdown Hall, Tetherdown N10 on Wednesdays at 17.00–19.00 from September to May. Even if you only know the basic moves, go along. You'll find you are welcome.

North London Chess Club has classes for beginners at Highbury Road School on Fridays 18.30–20.30. As soon as you've got a reasonable grasp of the game, you'll be moved on to play with adults who meet at Essex Road Library on Mondays 18.30–22.30.

Richmond and Twickenham Chess Club runs junior sessions for those aged 7–13 at the United Reform Church Hall, Quadrant Road, Richmond upon Thames.

Cinema

Most people know about Saturday morning cinema clubs. Entrance is quite cheap and details of the programmes will probably be in your local newspaper. To find out what is on at the main cinemas – ABC, Classic, Embassy and Odeon – ring Teledata 200 0200, or look in the *Evening Standard*. Children's cinema clubs have had something of a revival recently.

Cinemas and clubs

Barbican Centre has a children's cinema club on Saturday mornings at 11.00 and 14.30 for 6–12 year-olds. There are regular competitions and live entertainment. Membership is very cheap; day membership rather expensive.
● See also p.101.

Battersea Arts Centre shows children's films on Saturdays at 15.30.
● See also p.179.

Cartoon Classic Victoria is the only surviving cartoon cinema in England. Shows run from 12.00 every day.

ICA Children's Cinema Club has films on Saturday and Sunday afternoons at 16.00, and often matinées during school holidays – there's everything from space adventures to animation. There are also guest speakers and performers; badges, calendar wall charts and newsletters for members.

National Film Theatre's Junior NFT shows films for children on Saturday and Sunday afternoons.

Rio Centre usually selects films for children on Thursdays at 14.00, when it is packed with school parties with exams in mind. During school holidays there are films and cartoons for children.

Screen on the Hill has a Saturday Kids Club which offers 2½ hours of films and live entertainment for children of all ages every Saturday at 10.30. You have to be a member to get in.

Specialist Films

British Museum has film shows Tuesday–Friday at 15.30 on aspects of current and permanent exhibitions and other topics.
● See also p.56.

Commonwealth Institute shows free short films several times daily about Commonwealth countries.
● See also p.88.

Geological Museum shows free films during school holidays, and has regular performances and lectures Tuesday–Thursday and Saturdays at 14.30.
● See also p.156.

Imperial War Museum shows free films on Saturdays and Sundays. Under 12s must take an adult with them.
● See also p.42.

Museum of Mankind has film shows 11.30–14.30 Tuesday to Friday.

National Army Museum shows free films during school holidays.
● See also p.42.

National Maritime Museum shows free films in the Runciman Lecture Theatre in the holidays. Ring to find out what's on and the age group it's suitable for.
● See also p.55.

Science Museum shows children's films on Saturdays at 12.30.
● See also p.157.

Taking Part (see also Community centres)

Children's Film Unit (a Registered Charity) offers a unique opportunity to get involved in really professional film-making. The CFU has produced some excellent 16 mm films, and those involved in the production – actors, camera crew, lighting team, sound recordists, scriptwriters, set designers, co-ordinators and so on – are all youngsters (under 16) working under the supervision of expert film-makers.

Four Corners has two workshops for film, video, tape and script development, and its youth group meets on Mondays.

Inter-Action has a video club for 11s and over where you can make a video and watch video movies.
● See also p.78.

Museums

National Film Archive has a collection of films and recorded television programmes which illustrate the history of cinema and television. There's also a large collection of film stills, posters and set designs. Entry by appointment only.

Science Museum is the place to go if you're interested in how the cinema started. There's a good display of old cameras and projectors.
● See also p.157.

City farms

It isn't all that long ago when London had only one city farm. Now there are quite a lot. They all exist on land that was once thought to be useless, but which has proved to be productive. City farms all welcome help from children with feeding, grooming and mucking out and, in some cases, there's gardening too. Although the farms are free or very inexpensive to visit, donations are always welcome – animals, like children, aren't cheap to feed. If you are thinking of going in a group, remember to phone and give advance warning.

Organisation

National Federation of City Farms, The Old Vicarage, 66 Fraser Street, Windmill Hill, Bristol BS3 4LY, [Bristol 660663] has information about city farms throughout the country, and advises local groups on how to start similar projects.

Places to visit

Deen Farm Association, Batsworth Road, off Church Road, Mitcham, Surrey SW19, [648 1461] is a place where all are welcome. It's got lots of animals and birds, allotments and a garden, and it will soon have a covered indoor riding arena. Until it's in operation, it can only offer pony rides. The farm's open throughout the week 9.00–20.00 in the summer, and during daylight hours in winter.

Elm Farm, Gladstone Terrace, off Lockington Road SW8, [627 1130] is a particularly interesting place to visit. It's fairly new, and that means that if you are a regular visitor, you'll be able to see how a city farm develops. At the moment it's open at weekends 9.00–17.00, and all are welcome, especially if they help out with the goats, sheep, poultry, rabbits, donkeys and horses. Do remember that under 7s must take an adult along with them.

Freightliners Farm, Paradise Park, Sheringham Road N7, [609 0467] is closed on Mondays but open the rest of the week 9.00–13.00, 14.00–19.00, and until 18.00 in winter. Help is needed with its farmyard animals.

Hayes Hill Farm, Stubbins Hall Lane, Crooked Mile, Waltham Abbey, Essex, [Nazeing 2291] has a magnificent 16th-century barn, farmyard and paddocks. You can meet farm animals, walk to Holyfield Farm and stand in the viewing gallery and watch the dairy herd being milked. On Sundays there are often rural craft demonstrations.

Kentish Town City Farm, Cressfield Close, off Grafton Road NW5, [485 4585] is London's original city farm. Now it owns 75 farm animals and a goat dairy, and runs a full riding programme. There are also regular activities in the gardens and the chicken club. You can join its club, receive free copies of *City Farm News*, and have the chance to learn farm skills like milking, sheep shearing and animal care. (Canteen.)

Mudchute Community Farm, Pier Street E14, [515 5901] really was the site of a mud chute at one time. Now its 30 acres have been transformed into a productive farm with allotments, a wildlife area and a wet area, and it has an amphitheatre and a park with places where you can picnic. There's a flock of sheep and lambs, goats, cows, horses, rabbits, poultry, and an apiary, and it also runs a riding school. The farm is normally open during daylight hours.

Park Lodge Farm, Harvil Road, Harefield, Middlesex, [420 445] has occasional open days 11.00–18.00, when you can visit the dairy herd and sheep, watch milking, and visit the mobile zoo. There are always other displays and exhibitions about farming and the countryside. Normally, the farm's open to school parties who have made prior arrangements.

People's Farm, 108–122 Shacklewell Lane, Dalston E8, [806 5743] is happy to be visited by anyone of any age to see its animals, and to lend a hand with them. This farm is open 7 days a week 9.00–18.00.

Stepping Stones Farm, Stepney Way E1, [790 8204] covers 3½ acres and is open Tuesday–Sunday 9.30–13.00, 14.00–18.00. It houses cattle, sheep, goats, a pony and other animals, and it also has allotments. There's usually something going on during the holidays. At one time, with a bit of help, local children constructed a Wild West town. The farm is prepared to start classes in spinning and weaving if enough people are interested.

Vauxhall City Farm, 24 St Oswald's Place SE11, [582 4204] is open Tuesday–Thursdays and at weekends 10.30–17.30. Although all are welcome, local children can become members, help out with the work, and have pony rides, besides taking part in whatever play scheme is going on. Donkeys, ponies, goats, sheep, rabbits, poultry and a pig all live here.

Clocks

Why not go on a clock tour? London is full of clocks. After all, for centuries few people could afford to buy a watch, and so they were put on public buildings so that people could tell the time.

Indoor clocks

British Museum has an absorbing collection of clocks and watches dating from the 15th century. There's a clock shaped like a ship, an elaborate standing clock with figures that move and strike the hours, and many others.
● See also p.56.

Clockmakers' Company Museum is housed in the Guildhall. It's a fascinating collection, with astronomical clocks, a rolling ball clock, and a gas clock. There are lots of really beautiful watches, including a silver skull-shaped one which was owned by Mary, Queen of Scots.

J. Henry Schroder Wagg, merchant bankers, have a clock in their banking hall which you can see quite clearly from the street. In the centre of this modern clock is a small dial showing the time in England. The outside shows the time in the firm's branches all over the world.

Horniman Museum has the famous Apostle Clock. Stand in front of it at 16.00 and see the Apostles filing past Jesus. As they do so, they bow. Last in line is Judas, but as he approaches Christ, he turns back.
● See also p.106.

Old Royal Observatory has a large display of early astronomical and navigational instruments, clocks and sundials. Stand outside at 13.00 and look up at the turret. A red time ball will drop down the mast, something that has been going on since 1833. You can also stand on the meridian. If you put a foot on either side of the line, you'll be standing in both hemispheres at the same time. While you are there, have a look in the Meridian building at the permanent exhibition on time, its measurement, recording and distribution. (*See* National Maritime Museum.)

Science Museum shows the story of the measurement of time with water clocks, sundials, sand glasses, watches and chronometers. It also has the famous Wells Cathedral clock.
● See also p.157.

Sir John Soane's Museum has Sir Christopher Wren's silver watch and an orrery of 1773 showing the movement of the planets.

Victoria and Albert Museum has a large collection of clocks and watches, giving you a good idea of the history of timepieces. Among its exhibits are primitive methods of telling the time.
● See also p.139.

Wallace Collection has interesting clocks and watches on show, including an 18th-century regulateur which shows Greenwich mean time, real time, true solar time, the phases and ages of the moon, the rising and setting of the sun, and the date.
● See also p.48.

Outdoor clocks

Big Ben isn't actually the name of the clock on the Houses of Parliament. It's the bell that's called Big Ben, and it was named after Sir Benjamin Hall, the Commissioner of Works at the time. The clock itself is famous for its accuracy. Each of its four dials are 24 feet in diameter, the figures are 2 feet high, the big hand is 14 feet long, the small one 9 feet long, and the spaces between the minutes are a foot square.
● See also p.121.

Financial Times has a clock similar to that in Hampton Court (*see* below).

Fortnum and Mason's, in Piccadilly, sometimes has a small crowd waiting for the hour to strike on its famous clock which took 3 years to build and necessitated alterations to the shop. As the clock strikes 16.00, the 4-foot figures of Mr Fortnum and Mr Mason appear from the two pavilions. They move forwards, turn and face each other, and bow. As soon as the clock stops chiming, a series of 18th-century tunes are played on seventeen bells. The two gentlemen bow courteously to each other again and retire to their pavilions, and the doors close behind them.

Hampton Court Palace has a particularly interesting and beautiful clock. Stand in the Clock Court, and have a look. It was built for Henry VIII, and it tells the time, the date, how many days have passed in the year, the times of high water at London Bridge and the phases of the moon. In the centre, you'll see that the sun revolves round the earth. People at that time hadn't realised that it's the earth that revolves around the sun.
● See also p.145.

King's Cross station has a clock
on its tower which came from the
Crystal Palace after the Great
Exhibition of 1851. It's thought to
be a replica of the clock that stood
above the Tsar's stables in
Moscow.

Liberty's clock in Regent Street
has two panels, one to the right
and the other to the left. The
panel representing day has a
clock, and that representing night
has an owl holding a rat. In the
centre arch is St George and the
dragon. At a quarter past each
hour, St George chases the
dragon, while bells sound the
Westminster chimes. On the hour,
he chases the dragon four times,
and kills it with his lance as the
hour bell strikes.

St Dunstan-in-the-West stands on
the site of an early 13th-century
church. It was later rebuilt, and
then it was repaired in 1950.
Great care was taken to preserve
its famous lantern-steeple clock of
1671 with its striking jacks.

St Magnus the Martyr has a clock,
presented by Sir Charles
Duncomb, Lord Mayor of
London in 1708. As a poor
apprentice, he stood on London
Bridge in the early hours, waiting
for his master, but because he had
no way of telling the time, he
sometimes missed him. So, he
swore that when he became rich
and famous, he'd put up a clock
for the public, and so he did, and
this is it.

Coaches and carriages

You won't see many coaches or carriages on the streets of London these days, except on state occasions, although there are one or two firms who still use smartly painted cabs drawn by splendid horses, and you might just spot a brewer's dray with superb heavy horses. Nevertheless, there are a few places where you can go and admire them.

Places to visit

Gunnersbury Park Museum, once the home of the Rothschild family, has the coaches once owned by them. There's a heavy travelling chariot, used when they went to the Continent, a smart town chariot, painted in blue and yellow, and a hansom cab. You can also see a pony trap, a bath chair, and a tandem tricycle. (Tea pavilion in summer, weekends only in winter; picnic in grounds.)

Museum of London has a number of exhibits, including trade carts, but pride of place goes to the Lord Mayor's coach, an ornate, huge, gilded vehicle made in 1757, and brilliantly displayed. Nearby is a wonderful collection of saddlery.
● See also p.40.

Royal Mews has a fabulous collection of coaches, carriages, landaus and other horse-drawn vehicles. There's the Gold State Coach, which weighs 4 tons and is 24 feet long, and has to be drawn by 8 heavy horses, and you can see the Irish State Coach, the Glass Coach and others. The State Harness Room has liveries on display, and the Saddlery contains whips, saddles and embroidered saddle cloths. You can usually see the horses, but in the late summer and early autumn, many of them are sent on their summer hols to the country.

St Paul's Cathedral has the funeral carriage of the Duke of Wellington. It was so heavy that its 18 tons had to be drawn by 12 draught horses harnessed three abreast.
● See also p.123.

Science Museum has a number of early horse-drawn carriages, as well as an original mail coach.
● See also p.157.

Coins and medals

Lots of people collect coins and medals. Some are fascinated by them, others regard them as an investment. If you're interested, there are clubs and societies all over the country, and you'll find that they are usually very ready to give help and advice to those who are just starting a collection. Your local library might well have the address of a club in your area.

Museums

British Museum has a staggering collection of more than a million coins – not all on display at the same time. Serious students can see those in the Department of Coins and Medals, but there are lots to be seen in other departments.
● See also p.56.

Bruce Castle Museum has medals won by those who fought in the Middlesex Regiment.
● See also p.165.

Imperial War Museum has medals on display, including Victoria Crosses and George Crosses won by heroes of both World Wars.
● See also p.42.

National Army Museum's medals include Victoria Crosses won by soldiers during the battle of Rourke's Drift.
● See also p.42.

RAF Museum has a gallery devoted to holders of the Air Victoria Cross and the Air George Cross.
● See also p.33.

Royal Fusiliers Museum has the original Victoria Cross, struck for Queen Victoria's approval, and others won by members of the regiment.

Royal Hospital's museum has an astonishing display of about 1700 medals, most of them relics of past inhabitants of the Royal Hospital.
● See also p.111.

Verulamium Museum has lots of different Roman coins on display.
● See also p.41.

Community centres

Community centres are meeting places for the people who live in the area: places where they can go to join a club, learn a new skill or to use the facilities of the centre. They are often run and organised by the local people themselves, and everyone is welcome, from toddlers to pensioners. Many community centres have a crèche for babies so that Mum and Dad can enjoy themselves too.

There are community centres all over London – your local library or town hall will tell you if there is one near you. The ones listed here will give you an idea of the sort of activities you might find there.

Fleet Community Education Centre, Agincourt Road NW3, [485 9988] is open to anyone of any age who lives or works locally, and membership entitles you to go to any of the activities or use the facilities of the centre. There is a coffee bar, a pottery, a woodworkshop, a football pitch, a sewing room, a darkroom and a meeting hall. The play centre is open from Monday to Friday 16.30–18.00 for 5–11 year-olds, and there are all sorts of activities and outings during the holidays. For under 5s there is movement and drama; for 8–12s a dance drama workshop.

Gospel Oak Centre, 170 Weedington Road NW5, [485 2670] is for anyone up to the age of 16. For under 5s there's a nursery group every weekday; and for those between 5 and 16 there's the opportunity after school and on Saturdays to take part in music, drama, crafts, pottery, football, snooker, table tennis and netball.

Harmood Community Play Centre, 1 Forge Place, Ferdinand Street NW1, [482 2274] is open after school on Tuesdays, Wednesdays and Thursdays for children aged 5–11, and there are also activities in the school holidays. Art and craft, pottery, music, drama and dance are some of the things going on. One third of the group is mentally handicapped, and they integrate happily with other members.

Inter-Action Trust Centre, 15 Wilkin Street NW5, [485 0881] is a community centre for Kentish Town. There are clubs for gymnastics, drama, dance, as well as radio and computer camps. There is also a soft adventure playroom for under 5s, and a resource centre where you can use printing, video and media equipment. Prof. Dogg's Troupe, which works from the centre, is available for hire to other community groups. Inter-Action will also advise other centres about setting up computer camps.

Jackson's Lane Community Centre, 271 Archway Road N6 [341 1884] is alive with activity seven days a week from about 10.00. There's an art club, pottery, sports, a jazz music workshop and a film club. The theatre puts on some shows

specially for children – or you might be encouraged to participate, as happened when some puppeteers arrived! The centre caters for all ages.

Langdon Park Community Centre, Bright Street E14 has a wide range of both sporting and non-sporting activities on offer, including dance classes and band practice.

Last Chance Centre, 87 Masbro Road E14, [603 5581] provides activities and entertainment for people of all ages in the Hammersmith and Fulham area. 7–12 year-olds can do pottery,

judo, disco dancing, cycling workshop, camera club, games, swimming or drama after school and on Saturdays. For 12–18 year-olds there's a youth club. Club activities include darts, table tennis, pool, dominoes, five-a-side, basketball, netball and discos. During school holidays there is a special programme of sport, crafts, music and drama. The Family Bonanza Shows on Saturday afternoons are films and theatre for all the family.

Moonshine Community Arts Workshop, Victor Road NW10, [969 7959] is open most evenings for those living in Kensal Green. Over 14s can learn self-defence, and there's a video and sound workshop. For 10–12s Moonshine has a Super 8 animation work-shop which makes cartoons.

Conservation

(*see also* City farms, Natural history)

As people watch more and more buildings being erected and watch open spaces disappear and the destruction of yet more natural habitats, many have become aware of the need for conservation, and are determined to do something about it.

Organisations

British Trust for Conservation Volunteers, 2 Mandela Street NW1, [388 3946] has 35 groups active in London, but you have to be over 16 to join. It works on projects in London every week, and these range from the creation of wild gardens to turning an abandoned cemetery into a nature reserve. All you have to do is to make a phone call, and you'll be told about the work, where to meet, and what transport is available.

Ecological Parks Trust, Burlington House, Piccadilly W1, [734 5170] is open to anyone who supports its aims and objectives. It has already transformed derelict areas into places that support native species of plants that entice butterflies, insects, birds and wildlife to the area.

London Wildlife Trust, 1 Thorpe Close W10, [969 5368] manages several important reserves around London, and advises on the creation of nature parks on wasteland sites. Families can help on projects, take part in walks round London and attend lectures. Members receive a magazine four times a year.

WATCH, 22 The Green, Nettleham, Lincoln LN2 2NR, [0522 752326] is sponsored by the Royal Society for Nature Conservation and the *Sunday Times*, and is organised locally by Nature Conservation Trusts. Subscription is low, and in return you get a membership card, badge, and *Watchword*, its very lively magazine, three times a year with news of meetings, projects and competitions. You might find yourself involved in taking a butterfly census, taking part in tree planting schemes, going on a WATCH day outing or to a YHA/WATCH adventure holiday or weekend.

Wildlife Youth Service is a worthwhile organisation. Wildlife Rangers are aged 11–14, and the Panda Club is for those from 5–10. The club exists for all those interested in the countryside and its wildlife, and in wildlife in general.

Places to visit

Alexandra Park has a conservation area tucked away in one corner. There's a pond with small islands developed by the

London Conversation Volunteers, and these provide sanctuaries for nesting birds. There's a nature centre and interpretive plaques, and soon there'll be a nature trail.
● See also p.146.

Burgess Park is attracting world-wide attention. Although it's not complete, an area of 135 acres is being turned into a kind of nature reserve creating a natural habitat for native species of plants, birds and wildlife.

Dulwich Upper Wood SE19 is a 5-acre woodland nature reserve run by the Ecological Parks Trust. There's a warden, a teaching hut and an interpretive centre, and it's open Monday–Friday 10.00–18.00 or dusk.

Grebe House, St Albans, is a field study centre for the Hertfordshire/ Middlesex Nature Conservation Trust, and has a small display and a wildlife garden.

Lavender Pond, Rotherhithe Docks and the wetland behind it, is still being developed. The existing Old Pump House will soon be transformed into a teaching and interpretive centre.

Perivale Wood, Greenford, is a 27-acre nature reserve administered by the Selborne Society. It consists in the main of oak and hazelwood, and was once part of the ancient forest of Middlesex. Find out when its annual open day is. Usually it's in May when the woods are carpeted in bluebells.

William Curtis Ecological Park is a 2-acre site in Southwark. Although it's only been going for eight years, 350 species of plants and 250 species of animals have found a home there.

Museum

Natural History Museum has a permanent exhibition called Introducing Ecology, which helps you to understand the relation-ship and interdependence of living organisms.
● See also p.140.

Costumes

Not all old clothes are in museums. You can see quite a lot on the backs of people walking about. But they'll wear out eventually, so it's lucky that so many *are* preserved in collections.

Museums

Bethnal Green Museum of Childhood has a splendid collection of costumes dating back to 1700, many of them children's clothes. Don't miss the wedding dresses or accessories like hats, bags and shoes. You can look at Oriental costumes and materials at the same time.
● See also p.92.

Geffrye Museum has lots of costumes and accessories, many of them 19th-century women's and children's clothing.
● See also p.160.

Kensington Palace has life-size models in the state apartments, all wearing the kind of clothes that would have been worn at Court from the late 19th century onwards.
● See also p.145.

Museum of London has clothing dating from the 16th century, and houses the Royal Collection, which includes robes worn at three coronations, costumes belonging to Queen Alexandra and Queen Mary, and many other exhibits. In a quite different way, but equally splendid, is the costermonger suit which belonged to the Pearly King of Islington.
● See also p.40.

Museum of the Order of St John has a collection of clothes worn by members of St John's Ambulance Brigade, together with first aid kits, litters, medical instruments and other relics.

National Maritime Museum has clothes worn by sailors through the ages. There's the coat worn by Lord Nelson when he was killed at the battle of Trafalgar.
● See also p.55.

Salvation Army Museum shows the development of the movement with the aid of background music and informative tapes. You'll be able to see how the uniform has developed over the years and admire the famous bonnets.

Science Museum has an
exhibition called Clothes for the
Job. It shows all sorts of
specialised and protective
clothing, and includes flying, fire
and clean room wear.
● See also p.157.
Tower of London has gowns and
insignia of the Knights of the
Garter, Bath, Thistle and other
orders in the Jewel House.
● See also p.123.

Victoria and Albert Museum is
renowned for its huge collection
of clothes. Go straight to the
Costume Court, where clothes
and accessories from the late 16th
century to today are shown.
Elsewhere there are glittering
Oriental robes and magnificent
vestments on display.
● See also p.139.

Cricket

You're either keen on cricket, or
you're not. Most enthusiasts
support their local club, but if you
fancy going somewhere different,
try Blackheath, Chiswick Park,
Kew Green or Wimbledon
Common. Test matches, of
course, are held at Lord's and the
Oval. If you want to know the
latest test scores, telephone 160
from 8.00 to 19.00 Monday–
Saturday.

Organisations

Middlesex Cricket Union,
Secretary, 15 Sandstone, Kent
Road, Kew, Surrey, has
information about Middlesex
clubs.

National Cricket Association,
Lord's Cricket Ground, St John's
Wood NW8, [289 1611] is the
governing body, runs coaching
schemes and makes cricket
awards.

Cricket pitches

GLC parks with practice nets and
pitches that can be booked by
groups, are at Avery Hill,
Battersea Park, Bostall Heath and
Woods, Dulwich Park, Finsbury
Park, Hampstead Heath
Extension, Holland Park, Marble
Hill, Parliament Hill and Victoria
Park.

GLC parks with pitches but without practice nets are at Blackheath, Charlton Park, Crystal Palace Park, Eltham Park, Hainault Forest, Shrewsbury Park, South Hackney Marsh, Sutcliffe Park, Thamesmead, Weighall Road and Wormwood Scrubs.

Lambeth has cricket pitches at Brockwell Park, Clapham Common, Ruskin Park and Streatham Common. Telephone [622 6655, ext. 363] for bookings.

Southwark's pitches can be booked by application to the Sports Office, Plumstead Baths, Plumstead High Street SE18, [854 9217].

Coaching

Gover Cricket School, 172 East Hill SW18, [874 1796] operates throughout the year. Although not particularly cheap, it has excellent coaching and a lively social club.

Islington organises cricket coaching courses at the beginning of the summer holidays at Wray Crescent N4. Ring the Recreation Department, [607 7331] for details.

Lambeth Action Sports holds cricket practice sessions during the summer holidays with tuition by qualified cricketers. All you have to do is to turn up. Telephone [622 6655, ext. 325] for details.

Tower Hamlets Action Sports has coaching schemes during the summer holidays. Telephone [790 1818] for details.

Waltham Forest runs introductory and recreational cricket at Britannia Sports Ground, Billet Road E17, and Chingford Cricket Club offers advanced coaching. Telephone [521 7111] for information.

Museum

Cricket Memorial Gallery at Lord's has the Ashes and lots of cricketing relics, photographs and paintings, some interesting and some simply curious. It's open on match days and at other times by prior arrangement.
(Refreshments on match days, picnic in gardens at other times.)

Events (see Calendar)

Lord's Test Match

Oval Test Match

Cycling

London's hardly the best place in the world to go out for a carefree spin, so if you've got a bike or hope to own one, make sure you know how to ride and how to maintain it. If you live in west London, why not go along to the Last Chance Centre where the Brook Green Cycling Club operates. It has maintenance facilities, and you'll be offered expert help in keeping your bike in good condition, and the club also offers regular runs and trips out.

Organisations

British Cycling Federation, 16 Upper Woburn Place WC1, [387 9320] is more concerned with racing than touring. Once you've become a member, you'll get a useful handbook with information about clubs and cycling events.

Cyclists Touring Club, Cotterell House, 69 Meadrow, Godalming, Surrey, [Godalming 7217] has many clubs affiliated to it. It has details of clubs, offers advice on the care and safety of bikes, provides insurance cover, gives advice on touring at home and abroad, publishes a magazine 6 times a year, and organises adventure holidays.

Proficiency tests

These are run by many London boroughs. Get in touch with your local road safety officer or with ROSPA, 1 Grosvenor Crescent SW1, [235 6889] for details of programmes.

Hounslow organises cycling proficiency courses in the summer holidays, leading to the National Certificate and Badge award. Telephone [570 7728] for information.

Richmond upon Thames runs 5-day holiday courses. Telephone [943 1039] for details.

Waltham Forest organises summer holiday courses. Telephone [539 3650] for details.

Places to cycle

Canal towpaths may only be used by cyclists with permits. Contact British Waterways Board for information.

Crystal Palace National Sports Centre has a purpose-built cycle track.
● See also p.162.

Eastway Cycle Circuit at Eastway Sports Centre is a purpose-built 1.6 km circuit with facilities for racing and training, but you can also just ride for fun. There's coaching and competitions, and bikes for hire.

Herne Hill Stadium, off Half Moon Lane SE24, is used mainly for organised events, but when it's not in use, you can pay a small fee and use it.

Lordship Lane Recreation Ground has a mini-road system with lights, a one-way system, and so on. Don't worry if you haven't got a bike – you can borrow one.

BMX

If you are a BMX enthusiast, don't ride your bike in the street. It's dangerous, and a lot of young people have been killed or badly hurt. Furthermore, get yourself properly kitted out for this sport. Kidsline [222 8070] will know if there is a track in your area. The tracks at Eastway Sports Centre (*see* above) and at London Westway Freston Road W11, [969 0992] are considered among the best. At London Westway you can hire a bike.

Buying secondhand bikes

Markets selling secondhand bikes are at Kingsland Waste, Dalston, the north end of the Portobello Road by Golborne Road, and at Westmoreland Road, Walworth.

Hiring bikes

If you are under 18 and want to hire a bike, you'll have to be a competent rider and put down a hefty deposit, and you'll probably need a guarantee from your parents as well.

Broadway Bikes, 242 The Broadway NW6, [202 4671].

Dial-a-Bike, 2 Denbigh Mews, Denbigh Street SW1, [834 0756].

Fulham Cycle Store, 921 Fulham Road SW6, [736 8655].

London Bicycle Company, 41 Floral Street WC2, [836 7830].

Rent-a-Bike, 41–2 Floral Street WC2, [836 7830].

Savile's Cycle Stores, 97–9 Battersea Rise SW11, [228 4279].

Museums

British Motor Heritage Trust at Syon Park has tricycles and old bicycles on display.
● See also p.67.

Gunnersbury Park Museum has a tandem, a pennyfarthing and an old tricycle.
● See also p.76.

Science Museum has a good collection of old bikes. You'll soon see why the early ones were called bone-shakers.
● See also p.157.

Travelling with your bike

British Rail permits bikes to be carried free of charge on many of its Inter City trains and most of the London suburban services from Monday to Friday outside peak hour travelling times. In some cases, however, there are restrictions and/or a charge. Get hold of BR's pamphlet *Bike it by Train* to find out what they are.

Dance

Some people are naturally good at music and movement, but others seem to be just plain clumsy. However, even if you do seem to trip over your feet, don't despair. Not only are there places teaching every possible style of dance, but instructors claim that even the most elephant-like can learn to move really well.

Taking part

Battersea Arts Centre has ballet on Saturdays for 3–6 year-olds, 7–9 years and 10–12 years.
● See also p.179.

Dance Centre has classes in almost anything you can think of, from rock jazz to self-defence, taking in robotics, ballet, tap and so on. There is a very modest daily membership, and then you pay for each class, which lasts for one hour and starts on the hour.

Dance Works offers Saturday classes in classical ballet, tap and dance for 5–10 year-olds.

Greenwich Young People's Theatre has a modern dance workshop for those aged 14+. Music can be anything from rock and jazz to reggae and soul.
● See also p.169.

Hammersmith and Fulham have a Dance Fellow who coordinates and encourages dance projects, including jazz dance, tap, dancercise, and more, all for beginners and advanced dancers. Telephone [748 3020] for details of classes in your area.

Islington Dance Factory is a community arts centre specialising in music and dance. It has two large dance studios and a music studio and caters for 6–15 year-olds after school and on Saturdays. The dance classes are based on ballet technique, but this leads to workshops and dance performances, designing and making costumes.

Jenako Arts Multicultural Centre has African dance, drama and music for children as well as adults.

Pineapple Dance Studio has classes for 7–15 year-olds during the week and on Saturdays. There is a two-hour general class which includes acting, singing, dancing and voice production. Other classes are disco jazz, ballet, tap and basic jazz. You can either take out an annual membership – the best bargain – or pay daily.

Royal Academy of Dancing has classes for children from the age of 5 upwards who want to work through the grades examinations. On Saturdays there are classes specially for boys, with a male teacher. Entry to all classes is by audition only. The RAD runs one- and two-week summer schools which include classical dancing, dance composition, improvisation, folk dancing, mime, music and percussion.

Rudolph Steiner House offers eurythmy – the art of interpreting speech and music through movement – for small children on Saturday mornings.

Tower Hamlets Youth Dance Centre has Saturday morning classes in ballet and the Erick Hawkins Technique.

Young Place has Saturday classes for boys and girls aged 6 and over, a creative workshop for 10–12 year-olds; classes for 12–17s in contemporary dance and ballet, and workshops ending in studio performance. There are also holiday courses.

Watching

Ballet for All is part of the Royal Ballet Company. They tour for nine months of the year and run Young Place holiday courses.

Commonwealth Institute has ballet and national dance companies. These are usually lively and exicting performances. (Restaurant.)

Dance for Everyone is an enterprising young company trying to get children to express themselves in dance and mime. The group perform for clubs and schools, and in the Royal Festival Hall.

GLC puts on dancing in the open air at Battersea Park, Burgess Park, Eltham Park, Holland Park, Jubilee Gardens, Marble Hill and Victoria Park during the summer months.

London Coliseum stages ballet productions by foreign dance companies, and the London Festival Ballet's season each year, as well as the Nureyev Festival.

The Place is a contemporary dance theatre, putting on productions by experimental and foreign groups.

Royal Opera House is the home of the Royal Ballet Company, and for nine months of the year their productions alternate with those of the Royal Opera. There's always a huge demand for tickets, so book well in advance.

Sadler's Wells Theatre is the venue of visiting and foreign ballet companies.

Museums

Anna Pavlova Museum has mementoes of the life and career of one of the world's greatest ballet dancers.

Theatre Museum, opening in Covent Garden in 1986, will have a display illustrating the history of ballet, including the work of Diaghilev.

Day out

You will be using public transport on your day out – after all, unless you are going to the outskirts of London, your trip could be ruined if you're in a car. The traffic is dreadful, and parking is both difficult and expensive.

If you are going with a friend, make sure that between you you've got a good street guide, a map of the underground system and one showing bus routes. Don't forget that you can get cheap tickets for public transport. (*See* Travelling and sightseeing tours.)

You'll find hot-dog and ice-cream vans outside almost all major tourist attractions in central London. Be wary – they tend to be *very* expensive and not very good. Although it might seem a bore, you'll be much better off if you make yourself sandwiches and take some fruit with you and only use your money for drinks.

And you must remember to hang onto enough cash to ring your parents if you are likely to be late. You'll ruin *their* day if they are left sitting at home wondering what has happened to you.

Should you get lost, be sensible. Ask someone official like a policeman or traffic warden for help, or look for someone with a child in tow. If they've got a shopping basket, they'll probably be local and be most able to help you.

Central London

Travel: bus, tube
Visit: Pollocks Toy Museum; London Transport Museum; New Covent Garden (often free entertainment); National Gallery, National Portrait Gallery
Picnic: Embankment Gardens (a bit of a walk)
Eat: Refreshments in London Transport Museum and National Gallery; cafés and restaurants in New Covent Garden (not cheap); sandwich bars, cafés and restaurants nearby.

City of London 1

Travel: boat, bus or tube
Visit: Tower Bridge; HMS *Belfast*; Historic Ships Collection; Tower of London; brass rubbing centre and museum at All Hallows Barking-by-the-Tower
Picnic: Tower Wharf (not much room, not very comfortable)
Eat: cafeteria, snacks in Tower of London; sandwich bars, cafés and restaurants in area

City of London 2

Travel: (*see* above)
Visit: Museum of London; follow London Wall Walk; Barbican Centre; Telecom Technology Showcase; check on Molecule Theatre for performances
Picnic: Postman's Park
Eat: coffee shop in Museum of London; coffee shop and restaurants in Barbican Centre (not cheap); sandwich bars, cafés and restaurants in area

Greenwich

Travel: boat (highly recommended), BR
Visit: *Cutty Sark* and *Gipsy Moth IV*, National Maritime Museum and Old Royal Observatory (time visit in holidays for Greenwich Planetarium); Greenwich Park; wander round Greenwich
Picnic: Greenwich Park
Eat: coffee shop in National Maritime Museum; cafeteria in Cutty Sark Gardens, cafés in Greenwich

Kew and Brentford

Travel: boat (recommended), BR, bus
Visit: Kew Bridge Pumping Museum; Syon Park (Syon House, Butterfly House, British Motor Industry Heritage Trust); Music Museum
Picnic: gardens of Syon Park
Eat: cafeteria in Syon Park; cafés in Brentford High Street

Kew Gardens and old Brentford

Travel: boat (recommended), BR, bus
Visit: Kew Gardens and Kew Palace; Gunnersbury Park Museum; Gunnersbury Park (miniature golf, tennis, boating pond)
Picnic: Kew Gardens, Gunnersbury Park
Eat: cafeteria in Kew Gardens; tea pavilion in Gunnersbury Park (weekends only in winter)

Lee Valley Park

Travel: BR (Waltham Cross)
Visit: remains of Waltham Abbey and Epping District Museum (agricultural and craft displays, open Wednesday–Sunday afternoons); signposted country walk; Pickett's Lock Centre (roller skating, swimming and other sporting activities)
Picnic: picnic area at Waltham Abbey; countryside
Eat: refreshments at Pickett's Lock Centre

Richmond

Travel: Boat (recommended), BR, bus
Visit: wander round the green; visit antique, curio and craft shops in lanes and alleyways; hire a boat and go on the river; Ham House; skate at Richmond Ice Drome; check the programme at Marble Hill House (open air theatre, summer only)
Picnic: Terrace Gardens on the slopes of Richmond Hill, by the river
Eat: cafés and restaurants in the area

South Kensington
(an almost free day out)

Travel: Bus, tube
Visit: Geological Museum, Natural History Museum; Science Museum; Victoria and Albert Museum; walk in Hyde Park (time visit to see cavalry leaving or returning to Knightsbridge Barracks); Kensington Palace; the Serpentine for swimming or boating
Picnic: gardens of Natural History Museum; Hyde Park; Kensington Gardens
Eat: cafés and restaurants round South Kensington underground station (not cheap).

Westminster

Travel: Boat, bus, tube
Visit: Houses of Parliament; Westminster Abbey and Museum; Houses of Parliament; Jewel Tower; Imperial Collection
Picnic: St James's Park
Eat: not very good at Westminster, but sandwich bars, cafés and restaurants in nearby areas

Wimbledon

Travel: BR, bus, tube
Visit: Wimbledon Lawn Tennis Museum; Wimbledon Windmill Museum; Wimbledon Common; Polka Children's Theatre
Picnic: Wimbledon Common
Eat: cafés and restaurants in Wimbledon

Dolls and toys

Most of us have hung on to a battered old doll, a teddy bear with one eye or some other toy because it seems so heartless to throw them out. Some people, of course, kept their dolls and toys in really good condition, and a tremendous number of them have found their way into London's museums.

Organisations

Toy Libraries Association, Seabrook House, Darkes Lane, Potters Bar, Hertfordshire, [0707 44571] publishes *The Good Toy Guide*, a list of toys which have been assessed for safety, durability, play value and use.

Museums and exhibitions

Bethnal Green Museum of Childhood has a superb toy collection. There are dolls, many of them Russian, dolls' houses, rocking horses, puppets, optical toys, toy soldiers, miniature engines and penny toys, and so on. You can see model theatres, a peep show, and a real Punch-and-Judy booth. (Cafeteria nearby.)

Broomfield Museum has a replica of a Victorian nursery, with toys and games that would have been used by children at that time.
● See also p.140.

Cuming Museum has a small collection of toys bought at the Bartholomew Fair in 1849.
● See also p.40.

Horniman Museum gives you the opportunity to see toys from other countries.
● See also p.106.

Kensington Palace has the rooms used by Queen Victoria when she lived there as a child. Her Georgian dolls' house and other toys are on display.
● See also p.145.

London Toy and Model Museum is packed with toys of all kinds – mechanical toys, dolls, teddy bears, models and trains. You'll be amazed at the tin toys, which were bought for just one old penny.
● See also p.134.

Museum of London has dolls and toys of all periods, some of which belonged to Queen Victoria and Queen Mary when they were children. There are exhibits from the 18th and 19th centuries, and Queen Mary's dolls' house.
● See also p.40.

Pollock's Toy Museum consists of two inter-connected houses, and it really is a treasure trove. The exhibits are fascinating – Victorian toy theatres, nursery tableaux, dolls and dolls' houses, tin soldiers, board games, peep shows and optical toys, and the famous 'penny plain, tuppence coloured' Victorian toy theatre sheets.

Toy shops

Dolls' Hospital, 16 Dawes Road SW6, [385 2081]

Dolls' House, Unit 29, The Market, Covent Garden WC2, [723 1418]

Frog Hollow, 15 Victoria Grove W8, [584 5645]

Hamley's, 200 Regent Street W1, [734 3161]

James Galt, 30 Great Marlborough Street W1, [734 0829]

Kristin Baybars, 3 Mansfield Road NW3, [267 0934]

Oscar's Den, 127 Abbey Road NW6, [328 6683]

Playgear, 3 Dennis Parade, Winchmore Hill Road N14, [882 1293]

Singing Tree, 69 New Kings Road SW6, [736 4527]

Tiger, Tiger, 219 Kings Road SW3, [352 8080]

Toy Cave, 267 Chiswick High Road W4, [994 5374]

Tree House, 237 Kensington High Street W8, [937 7497]

Tridas Toy Shop, 44 Monmouth Street WC2, [240 2369]

Famous people

So many famous people have lived in London, that it's not easy to decide who to put in and who to leave out. In some cases, their houses have become museums, in others there are only relics or statues to look at.

Blue plaques

As you stroll around London streets, you'll see that some buildings have blue plaques on them. They are put up by the GLC to show where famous people have lived or worked. Now there are over 400, commemorating people connected with the arts, politics, science and the armed forces. You'll see that sometimes they are quite close together. That's because people like artists and writers often chose to live close to each other.

Faces

Madame Tussaud's exhibition in Baker Street is the famous waxworks which has a collection of the famous and the infamous, both the living and the dead. It goes to enormous trouble to get details right – clothes, buttons, the way shoes are laced, and that sort of thing.

Its Royalty and Railways exhibition at Windsor and Eton Central Railway station is a must. There's the *Queen*, a marvellously reconstructed 1894 steam locomotive with royal guests aboard the train preparing to meet Queen Victoria, and the Guard of Honour saluting the Queen and her guests as they leave the fully restored Royal Waiting Room. There's also an astonishing theatre show presenting outstanding events of the Queen's reign. At the end, the Queen and famous Victorians come to life, actually talking and moving in a series of events.

National Portrait Gallery doesn't sound too lively, but if you go in, you'll soon change your mind. Some of its 9000 portraits are magnificent, but some aren't. It's the face that matters, not the artist. It's now got a new gallery of Tudor portraits, and you shouldn't miss the 20th-century galleries with paintings, drawings, sculpture and stunning photographic material.

 (*See* National Gallery.)

Westminster Abbey Museum has fascinating effigies of people. They used to be carried in funeral processions, and were made in a variety of materials – wood, leather and wax. The oldest is a wooden one of Edward I, and the oldest wax effigy is that of Charles II. That of Queen Elizabeth I isn't the original. It's a copy, made in the 18th century.

● See also p.122.

Houses and graves

Baden-Powell House gives you a good idea of the life of Lord Baden-Powell, the founder of the Scout movement.

Carlyle's House, the home of the author for 47 years, is in Chelsea. Most of the furniture was his, and there are books, pictures, letters and manuscripts. It's as if he might stroll in at any moment. Go there on a bright day, since some of the rooms are without electricity. Not far away, in Embankment Gardens, is a statue of him gazing thoughtfully across the river.

Geoffrey Chaucer, who wrote *The Canterbury Tales*, lived in Fish Street in the City of London, was married in the Royal Chapel of the Savoy, and is buried in Westminster Abbey. His burial place was chosen at random, but the area has since become known as Poet's Corner.

Charles Dickens lived for only a couple of years in the house in Doughty Street, but such a marvellous atmosphere has been created, that it feels as if he'd been there all his life. There's lots to look at, and in the basement is a super recreation of the Dingley Dell kitchen.

Hogarth's House, in Chiswick, has many examples of the artist's prints, personal relics, books and furniture of the period.

Dr Johnson's House is a 17th-century building where he compiled his great dictionary, which you can see as you enter the house. There are portraits of his contemporaries, and many relics. His summer house, which was moved from Streatham, is now to be seen at Kenwood. There's a statue of him, draped in a toga, in St Paul's Cathedral, and another outside St Clement Dane's, the church he attended. Inside you'll see a brass plate marking his pew.

John Keats' Museum is in Hampstead. You can see his relics and those of some of his friends, and there are lots of books, manuscripts and letters to gaze at.

Lord Nelson is buried in the crypt of St Paul's. His coffin was made from the mainmast of a captured French ship. The black marble sarcophagus was intended for Cardinal Wolsey, who died about 280 years earlier. The cardinal was out of favour with the king at the time, and Henry VIII thought it too good to be used for him, so it hung around until a suitable recipient was found. Nelson's effigy is in Westminster Abbey Museum.

- See also p.123.

Karl Marx has a tomb in Highgate cemetery. It's huge and hideous. You can't possibly miss it.
- See also p.106.

Samuel Pepys, whose diaries give such a vivid picture of the London of his day, is buried in St Olave's, Hart Street, where you can see effigies of him and his wife. Ivory chessmen, backgammon counters and draughts, said to be given to him by James II, are in the Museum of London.

John Wesley's House and Chapel is an 18th-century house opposite Bunhill Burial Fields. It contains furniture, books and other relics. The chapel is next to the house, and behind it is the graveyard where he is buried.

Dick Whittington, three times Lord Mayor of London, 'turned again' on Highgate Hill, where a stone marks the spot. He was buried in St Michael's, Paternoster, but his body was dug up by a verger who thought that treasure was buried with it. Actually, Dick Whittington built the original church. When the present church was being restored, a mummified cat was found in it.

Statues

Prince Albert, the husband of Queen Victoria, has a memorial, thought by many to be quite hideous but loved by others. It's opposite the Royal Albert Hall. What he is clutching in his hand is a catalogue of the Great Exhibition of 1851, his brainchild.

Charles I's superb statue is on the south side of Trafalgar Square. It was removed during the Commonwealth, and sold to be melted down. Sure enough, the man who bought it sold knives and other souvenirs supposed to be made from the metal, but at the Restoration, he produced the statue again. The wily brazier, no doubt a rich man by then, had hidden it in his garden.

● See also p.123.

Elizabeth I, together with King Lud and his sons, used to stand at Lud Gate, one of the entrances to the City. When the gate was demolished, they were taken to St Dunstan-in-the-West. The Queen stands regally over the door, the others are inside.

● See also p.75.

Richard the Lionheart can be seen in Old Palace Yard. The monument has reliefs showing what happened to the king. He was badly wounded by an arrow. The archer who shot him was captured and taken to the dying monarch. However, Richard pardoned him, but most unfairly, as the king breathed his last, his nobles grabbed the archer, who was expecting to go free, and had him flayed alive.

Fire

One of the greatest fears of the City of London was that of fire. In medieval and Tudor times, buildings were constructed of timber, and they were huddled so closely together that fire spread very quickly.

Rules were made about buildings, but these were usually ignored. Then, in 1666, came real disaster – the Great Fire. It started in Pudding Lane and ended at Pie Corner – a punishment for London's gluttony, they said. It lasted for 5 days, consumed St Paul's Cathedral, the Guildhall, the Royal Exchange, the Customs House, 87 parish churches and hundreds of other buildings. It made thousands homeless and completely destroyed an area of 373 acres within the City and 63 acres outside it.

London was devastated again during the Second World War. It was heavily bombed and thousands of incendiary bombs started huge fires, but just as they had in 1666, Londoners simply picked themselves up and started to rebuild their City once again.

Places to visit

Chartered Insurance Institute Museum has a huge collection of British and foreign fire marks. These badges were fixed to the walls of buildings insured by early companies against fire risk. These companies ran their own private fire brigades. If a fire broke out, the firemen went out and had a look. If the mark on the wall of the building didn't belong to their company, they simply went home again.

These early firemen were not professionals. They were usually watermen, and there is a selection of their badges and helmets on display. Well worth seeing are three old fire engines and a 19th-century pump.

Cock Lane has a gilt figure of a boy marking the point where the fire stopped.

Gunnersbury Park Museum has a fire engine of 1870.
● See also p.76.

Monument was erected as a memorial to the Great Fire. On the very top there's an urn with a flaming ball. Look at the bas reliefs on the base. There are Latin inscriptions on three sides naming some of the fire fighters of the time. On the fourth side is Charles II, looking as if he's protecting the City. A lady in the corner doesn't seem all that convinced.

When the fire broke out, and for some time afterwards, it was thought to have been started by Roman Catholics. The inscription on the Monument blaming them has, quite rightly, been obliterated. The poet Pope, writing of the Monument when it was still there, wrote:

Where London's column pointing to the skies,
Like a tall bully, lifts its head and lies—

Museum of London has a stunning model of the City of London in 1666. As you look at it, you'll see a small fire breaking out and then growing bigger and bigger until it engulfs the City. Although the show only lasts a few minutes, it's very impressive. There are light and sound effects, and even gusts of hot air. The Museum also possesses a stone slab which had been placed at Pudding Lane repeating the old Roman Catholic conspiracy theory, and there's a horse-drawn fire engine of 1862.
● See also p.40.

St Paul's, on its south front pediment, has a phoenix, a bird that was supposed to be consumed in fire, but which rose again afterwards, renewed. It recalls the moment when Sir Christopher Wren, who was rebuilding the cathedral, asked a workman to bring him a stone to mark the exact centre of the dome. What was handed to him was a piece of tombstone with the word *Resurgam* on it. It means 'I shall rise again'.
● See also p.123.

Science Museum shows devices for making fire and for putting it out. It has the Bryant and May collection, fire engines, one of them built in 1734, a modern turntable ladder 100 feet high, and appliances, alarms and sprinklers.
● See also p.157.

Fishing

For centuries people fished in the Thames, but by the 19th century the river had become so polluted that MPs had to take defensive action. All the apertures in the Houses of Parliament were filled with sacking soaked in disinfectant. Slowly, over the years, conditions improved, but still few fish were able to survive. However, the river's been cleaned up, and well over 100 different species of fish have been found, and in 1984 the first salmon was caught in the Thames.

Places to see fish

Chessington Zoo has an aquarium.
● See also p.37.

Horniman Museum has tanks of fish and other water creatures.
● See also p.106.

London Zoo has a very large aquarium.
● See also p.37.

Where to fish

Barn Elms Reservoirs: 3 waters for trout fishing (15 March – 30 November). Day permits and part day permits can be bought at the gatehouse but only a limited number of tickets are issued, so it will be a good idea to ring first and find out if there are any left. Telephone [748 3423 or 837 3300] for advance bookings.

Kempton Park West Reservoir: permits available from the gatekeeper or in advance from Thames Water (Metropolitan Division), New River Head, Roseberry Avenue EC1 [837 3300].

River Lee: several areas have been set aside for day ticket fishing. From Tottenham to Cheshunt, fishing is free. For further information, contact Thames Water (Lee Division), The Grange, Crossbrook Street, Waltham Cross, Hertfordshire or Lee Valley Regional Park, Enfield, Middlesex.

River Thames: all fishing on tidal stretches of the river is free. You can fish from any suitable place on the banks, except round locks or where the gardens of private property run down to the river.

Thames Water Area: everyone aged over 12 needs a rod licence for fishing in Thames Water rivers and reservoirs. This can be bought at fishing tackle shops or by post from Thames Water, Nugent House, Vastern Road, Reading, [Reading 593538].

Walthamstow Reservoir: 10 different waters for coarse fishing, 2 for trout. Permits for whole, part day or evening at the reservoir, or buy a permit for the season. Under 16s must be accompanied by an adult.

Lake and pond fishing

You can fish for free and without a permit in the following places:

Battersea Park; Burgess Park; Clapham Common (Mount Pond, Eagle Pond); Clissold Park; Cray Valley, Bexley (Five Arches Meadow); Epping Forest Ponds; Finsbury Park; Hainault Forest; Hampstead Heath Ponds; Highgate Ponds; Keston Ponds, Bromley; Mitcham Common (Seven Islands Pond, One Island Pond); Stanmore Common Ponds; Tooting Common; Victoria Park; Wandsworth Common.

For the following, you need a permit. If you apply in writing, do it on or soon after 1 April, but don't leave it too late since there's a limited number of season permits available:

Brooklands Lake, Dartford: permits from bailiff on bank.

Bushey Park Ponds, Hampton Court Ponds (Long Water, Willow, the Rick): apply in writing to Superintendent of Parks, Hampton Court Gardens, East Molesey, Surrey.

Cannon Hill Common Road, Bushey Mead: permits from bank.

Crystal Palace Boating Lake: permits from bank.

Danson Park Lake, Bexley: permits from bank.

Horton Kirby Lakes, Dartford: permits from bailiff on bank.

Osterley Park Lake: apply in writing to the Superintendent of Parks, Hyde Park W2.

Richmond Park Ponds: apply in writing to the Superintendent of Parks, Bog Lodge, Richmond Park, Surrey.

Ruislip Lido: permits on site.

Ruxley Lakes (Footscray): limited day tickets on weekdays obtainable in advance from tackle shop in St Mary Cray.

Serpentine Lake: apply in writing to the Superintendent of Parks, Hyde Park W2.
● See also p.148.

South Norwood Lake: permits from bank.

Thamesmead: permits on bank.
● See also p.31.

Trent Park Lake: permits on bank.

Canals

Grand Union Canal is controlled by the London Anglers Association, 183 Hoe Street E17, [520 7477]; permits available from bailiff on the bank.

Regent's Canal is fished by the Camden Raven Angling Club; very cheap subscription for Camden residents under the age of 16.

Docks

Shadwell Basin Project is in the old London Docks and offers angling among its many activities. Telephone [481 4210] for information.
● See also p.65.

South East London Aquatic Centre at Woolwich Dockyard has an angling dock. Telephone [855 0131] for information.

Surrey Docks: permits available on site.

Flowers and plants

(*see also* Parks)

Londoners really are lucky. There are lots of parks and gardens and charming little squares, many with stunning displays of flowers and shrubs.

Advice on Gardening

Avery Hill Park Gardens have occasional open days when you can visit its nursery and talk to the staff. Ring [850 2666] for information.
● See below.

Horniman Gardens run Gardening for Children. It meets on occasional Wednesdays in the holidays 14.30–15.30, and there are talks and demonstrations about things like planting window boxes or how to take cuttings. If it's wet, it all goes on in the Dutch barn. Telephone [633 1707] for information.

Gardens to visit

Avery Hill Park Winter Gardens are a kind of mini-Kew. There are three plant houses – cool, temperate and tropical with lots of unusual plants, many of them from Australia and Asia.

Barbican Centre has a magnificent conservatory on level 8 with a stunning display of plants. It's open Monday–Saturday 10.00–18.00, and Sunday 12.00–18.00. (Refreshments, lunch, dinner.)

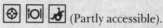 (Partly accessible).

Brockwell Park, an old flower garden in Stockwell, was once the kitchen garden of a mansion. Its yew hedges are very old, and it has a number of unusual flowers and trees.

Chelsea Physic Garden is London's oldest botanical garden. It dates back to 1673 when the Worshipful Company of Apothecaries moved because they thought the City was too polluted. The garden consists of about 4 acres and it has round about 5,000 different plants.

Chiswick House Garden was laid out by Lord Burlington and William Kent. It's a lovely place to go, with superb vistas, water, bridges, temples and statues.
● See also p.120.

Hampton Court Palace has something for everyone – a knot garden, the great vine, the maze, old-fashioned sweet-smelling flowers and wonderful landscaped gardens.
● See also p.145.

Holland Park has 55 acres of lawns and 28 acres of woodland. There's an Irish garden, a rose garden and the Dutch garden which must be seen in the spring

when it's ablaze with tulips.
● See also p.148.

Kew Gardens is really called the Royal Botanical Gardens, and dates from 1759 when Princess Augusta decided to have a few acres planted, but somehow it went on growing. It has thousands of trees, shrubs and plants.

The Palm house has about 45,000 square feet of glass, and it's heated for its collection of tropical plants. Alas, it seems as if it will have to be renovated soon. The Chinese Pagoda, dating from 1761, is 10 storeys high and 163 feet tall, but there's nothing in it except a staircase. There are acres of lawn, lovely flowers, and walks down to the riverside.

The Queen's garden has been laid out as it would have been in the 17th century, and has only plants available at the time. There's a bowered pergola walk with lots of herbs, all carefully labelled with suitable literary quotations. (Snacks.)

Regent's Park is always a pleasant place to go for a stroll. Queen Mary's rose garden mustn't be missed. It's charming, with lovely little bowers lining the edges of the garden and with roses climbing up the walls.
● See also p.149.

Syon Park has 53 acres of garden with lakeside walks and woodland. It's glorious in the summer with thousands of roses to admire and smell. The 1820 conservatory has indoor plants, cacti and orchids, and small birds dart about the greenery.

● See also p.67.

Westminster Abbey has the oldest garden in London – it's been there for over 900 years.
● See also p.122.

Museum

Museum of Garden History is in St Mary's Church on the east side of Lambeth Bridge. The Tradescants, father and son, were the 17th-century royal master gardeners and are buried in the churchyard which has been turned into a charming 17th-century garden.

Events (see Calendar)

Westminster Cathedral Spring Flower Festival

Spring Flower Show

Chelsea Flower Show

Royal National Rose Society Show

Late Autumn Show

City of London Flower Show

Folk

There are a number of folk clubs in London where older people can spend the evening listening to music, but as these come and go so quickly there is no point in listing them here. The following events are fairly permanent fixtures.

Organisation

English Folk Song and Dance Society has a children's section called the Hobby Horse Club. Members receive a badge, a birthday card, newsletters, a list of festivals where there will be children's events, and holidays are organised from time to time. Occasionally dances are held on Saturday afternoons at Cecil Sharp House, as well as a Christmas party.

Those aged 11–18 can become youth members of the Society, and each Saturday night there is either a dance or folk music, and the occasional tea dance in the afternoon. There is also a Saturday Folk Cellar Club, and sometimes events on other nights during the week.

Cecil Sharp House has a folk shop which is open 9.30–17.30, later on Saturdays, and the Vaughan Williams Memorial Library, where occasional lectures are held.

GLC folk concerts

GLC puts on folk concerts and dancing during the summer months. Look out for these events in Battersea Park, Burgess Park, Eltham Park South, Holland Park, Jubilee Gardens, Marble Hill Park and Victoria Park.

Event (*see* Calendar)

English Folk Song and Dance Society Festival

Football

Football fans are well catered for, whether they want to play or watch. Although the season lasts from September to April, you can find somewhere to kick a ball around every day of the year.

Organisations

Football Association, 16 Lancaster Gate W2, [262 4542] is the governing body of the sport and organises coaching schemes for talented young people.

London Youth Football Association, [987 3544] (evenings only) will help you to find a club near you if you're really stuck, but first try your local sports centre or ask at your local library.

GLC has pitches in many London parks and organises free daytime group instruction during the summer holidays. Telephone [633 1708] for details.

Playing

Almost all sports centres offer 5-a-side football as one of their activities. Some do more, with junior football clubs and coaching by FA coaches.

Bullsmoor Sports Centre has a junior football clinic on Tuesday evenings. FA registered coaches teach the skills of heading, dribbling, passing, goalkeeping, shooting and so on. There's also extra coaching in the school holidays.
● See also p.162.

Michael Sobell Sports Centre has junior football coaching after school. Its junior football club aims to field three teams – under 13s, under 15s, and under 17s, to be coached by registered FA coaches in intensive Saturday training sessions.
● See also p.163.

Tottenham Sports Centre has junior football coaching after school. There are two groups, one for those aged 5–8, the other for 9–12 year-olds.
● See also p.163.

Tower Hamlets Community Sports includes football in its school holiday sports activities. Telephone [790 1818, ext. 269] for information. Its Action Sports Team runs two teams, one for those under 16 and one for those aged 16 and over, and it's also setting up an Unemployed Football League. Telephone [247 1286] for information.

Watching football

If you want a seat, postal bookings are accepted 21 days before a match. Otherwise you can turn up and queue to stand on the terraces. It's best to get there by 14.00 – kick off is at 15.00.

Arsenal, Arsenal Stadium, Avenell Road N5, [359 0131]

Brentford, Griffin Park, Ealing Road, Brentford, [560 2021]

Charlton Athletic, The Valley, Floyd Road SE7, [858 3711]

Chelsea, Stamford Bridge Grounds, Fulham Road SW6, [385 5545]

Crystal Palace, Selhurst Park, Whitehorse Road SE25, [653 4462]

Fulham, Craven Cottage, Stevenage Road SW6, [736 6561]

Leyton Orient, Leyton Stadium, Brisbane Road E10, [539 2223]

Millwall, The Den, Cold Blow Lane SE14, [639 3143]

Queen's Park Rangers, Rangers Stadium, South Africa Road W12, [743 0262]

Tottenham Hotspur, White Hart Lane, 748 High Road N17, [808 1020]

West Ham United, Boleyn Ground, Green Street E13, [470 1325]

Tour

Wembley Stadium offers behind-the-scenes tours of the changing rooms and the chance to enter the pitch through the players' tunnel to the sound effect of crowds roaring. You can climb the steps to the Royal Box and imagine how it must feel to those lucky few who have made it to the top. There's also a display of cups and medals, pictures of the first Cup Final, and a slide show.

Event (*see* Calendar)

FA Cup Final

Ghosts, gibbets, graveyards and gruesome places

All sorts of horrific things have happened in London – people have been tortured, burned and executed, and hung, drawn and quartered. Although it's a long time since anything as gruesome as that has happened, many places where they were carried out are still there. We've included places where ghosts have been reported, but we can't promise that they'll materialise for you.

Places to visit

Adelphi Theatre has an elegant ghost. A famous Victorian actor was murdered in 1897, and he's said to be seen stalking up and down Covent Garden tube station in a very theatrical way.

All Hallows Barking-by-the-Tower shows in its church register of 1665 that 94 people of the

parish died painfully of the plague in September of that year.
● See also p.40.

British Museum has a large collection of mummies and mummy cases, the earliest of about 4500 BC, and the mummies of sacred animals. There's also a reconstruction of a Greek tomb which is 20 feet high.

The museum is also reputed to have a ghost. As you might expect, she's an Egyptian princess.
● See also p.56.

Brompton Cemetery has some extraordinary tombs and memorials, some astoundingly ugly. Alas, many of the tombstones have toppled over, adding to its dismal air of neglect.

Cuming Museum houses the Lovatt collection of London superstitions. Oak-apples, strung like a necklace and worn round the neck, were a means of keeping sore throats at bay.

Elephant and Castle tube station has unexplained strange noises – running footsteps, knockings and tappings.

Gibbets, where people were publicly hanged, were regarded with dread. People who had to go past, crossed themselves and muttered prayers. Even so, a public hanging brought crowds in their thousands to watch. Tyburn Tree was easily the most famous, and this is marked by a small tablet on the park side of Marble Arch. Blackheath, Charlton Heath and Wimbledon Common all had gibbets.

Hampton Court Palace has a haunted gallery. Two queens, both wives of Henry VIII, are said to walk there. One is sad Jane Seymour, who died after giving birth to a son, and she holds a lighted taper in her hand. The other is a distraught Catherine Howard, who was executed by the king. She rushes towards the Chapel as she did just before she was taken to the Tower of London, hoping that if she could see her husband, he would relent. Alas, guards stopped her from seeing him.
● See also p.145.

Highgate Cemetery is a curious place. It's overgrown, and always feels damp. There are amazing memorials, Egyptian-type catacombs and huge vaults, and broken tombstones reel drunkenly about. Lots of famous people are buried here – Faraday, George Eliot and Rosetti among others. There are occasional open days on Sundays from 13.00–17.00, with members of the preservation society to guide you. Look in the national and local press for details.

Horniman Museum has an ancient Egyptian tomb, the skeleton surrounded by pots and weapons, and quite a collection of mummies. Its Cult of the Dead section also has mummified bodies. There's also an iron torture chair used in 17th-century Spain. (Tea room, afternoons

only; Horniman gardens,
refreshments in summer only.)

Kensal Green Cemetery, founded
in 1822, covers 56 acres. Coffins
could be taken there by barge
through the watergates. Like most
large cemeteries, parts appear
very neglected now.

Kensington Palace is supposed to
have the ghost of poor Princess
Sophia, the blind daughter of
George III. Even if you don't see
her, you might hear the hum of
her spinning wheel.
● See also p.145.

Lincoln's Inn Fields was used for
executions, and fourteen people
found guilty of conspiring to
assassinate Elizabeth I died there.
There are stories of voices crying
out in the night, but no sighting of
ghosts.

London Dungeon is not the place
to go if you are squeamish or
nervous. It gives a detailed and
comprehensive view of horrific
murder, torture, demonology and
witchcraft. There are vile, slimy
vaults, and its special lighting and
sound effects are hair-raising.
Unaccompanied children, quite
rightly, are not admitted.
(Refreshments.)

Madame Tussaud's, apart from
its famous waxworks, has the
Chamber of Horrors, which
depicts hideous crimes and

executions using the guillotine,
the rack and other instruments of
torture. There are now excellent
reproductions of the alleys and
courts of Jack the Ripper's
London.
● See also p.93.

Museum of London has wooden
debtors' cells from Wellclose
Square with the names of some of
their occupants carved on them.
The doors to the cells actually
came from Newgate prison.
There's an iron corpse cage.
That's where the bodies of
executed criminals were placed
for public display.
● See also p.40.

National Army Museum has the
saw used to hack off the leg of the
Earl of Uxbridge. He'd probably
have been conscious while it was
done.
● See also p.42.

St Bartholomew's Hospital has
memorials to Protestant martyrs
on its hospital wall, burned to
death in June 1558. During
mid-19th century excavations,
blackened stones and bones were
found, together with the remains
of posts and rings.

St Boltoph's is reputed to have
the head of the Duke of Suffolk.
It's said that ages ago a verger
began sawing up coffins for fuel,
and he probably used the duke's.
Anyway, the vaults were sealed
up. Much later, in 1851, when
they were reopened, a head was
found in a heap of sawdust, which
probably preserved it. The neck
has more than one wound.

Obviously, the executioner wasn't very good at his job.

St Thomas's Operating Theatre used to be part of the chapel of St Thomas's hospital and was in use 1861–2. Now it has been converted into a museum. You've only got to take one look to see how grisly operations must have been in those days.

Sir John Soane's Museum has the cell of an imaginary monk, catacombs and a Sepulchral Chamber with Seti I's alabaster sarcophagus.

● See also p.73.

Theatre Royal, Drury Lane has a white-wigged, well-dressed ghost who carries a sword. Usually he sits in the fourth row of the upper circle, moves across the gangway, and disappears through a wall. Thoughtfully, he's never there after 18.00, so theatre-goers are never embarrassed by sitting on him. Oddly enough, in Victorian times, workmen broke through a wall and found a small room with the skeleton of a man in it, a dagger still in his ribs. The body was buried in the nearby Drury Lane Gardens.

Tower of London, once a place of fear, has many relics. There's Traitors' Gate, through which Elizabeth I walked when still a princess, loudly protesting her innocence. You can see the spot where executions were carried out. The aged Countess of Salisbury refused to be executed, and sparked off a grisly chase with the executioner – he won. You can see instruments of torture in the Bowyer Tower.

● See also p.123.

Trinity Square is the site of the old Tower Hill scaffold. Lord Lovat, the last man to be executed there, almost died of laughing as the spectators' stand collapsed, killing twelve onlookers.

Westminster Abbey has the ghost of a monk who haunts the precincts. His feet glide along above the level of the paving. The reason is obvious. The slabs have become worn away with the passage of time, so the monk actually walks on what was the correct level.

● See also p.122.

Guided tours

(*see also* Travelling and sightseeing tours, Walks)

It's always interesting to see what's going on behind the scenes and to find out how things work. Quite a lot of businesses and organisations offer conducted tours of their premises.

Business world

Baltic Exchange is an important exchange and shipping market, where deals are made over ships and cargoes. Parties of not more than 20 are shown around on Wednesdays and Thursdays 11.30–12.30. Write to the Secretary well in advance.

Lloyds is an international insurance market and the centre of shipping intelligence. It's open on working days, with 30-minute tours at 1.00 and 14.30, to those over the age of 17 or in a sixth form, and the party should number 15. Write 3–4 months in advance to J. F. Hutcheon in the Information Department.

Stock Exchange is the place to go to watch 2,000 well-dressed men and women beavering away. Guides give talks, and you can see a film in the adjoining gallery. By the time you leave, you should have some idea of what the financial world is all about.

Newspapers

Daily Express takes groups of 12 over the age of 16 on a tour on Sundays and Mondays from 2.30 and on Saturdays at 19.30. Write at least 5 months in advance to the Group General Manager.

Daily Mail takes groups of 12 people over the age of 14 on Tuesdays and Wednesdays 21.00–23.15. Write at least 6 months in advance to the General Production Manager.

Daily Telegraph takes groups of 8 people over the age of 13 on Mondays, Tuesdays and Fridays 20.45–22.45. Write at least 6 months in advance to Visits Department.

Post offices

Parties should not include anyone under the age of 14, although in certain cases and in particular the case of the National Postal Museum, exceptions might be made. Applications should be made at least 3 months in advance.

Croydon Head Post Office is the centre for letters and parcels posted and delivered in the area. Visiting times throughout the year (not December) are Tuesday–Thursday 14.30–16.30 and 18.00–19.30. Parties should not exceed 20 in number. Apply to the Head Postmaster, Planning and Mechanisation Section, 1–5 Addiscombe Road, Croydon CR9 6AB, [688 3651, ext. 251].

King Edward Building is chiefly concerned with London and overseas letters. Organised visits include the sorting offices and the underground railway, and last about 2 hours. It's open throughout the year (not December) Monday–Thursday 10.30–16.00. Parties should not exceed 20, and written application should be made several weeks in advance to the Postmaster Controller, King Edward Street, EC/FS (S & B Branch), EC1 1AA, [601 9219].

London Overseas Mail Office sorts parcels going overseas or coming from abroad. Visits last about 90 minutes and take place Monday–Friday 10.00–15.00. Parties should not exceed 20, and written application should be made in advance to The Manager, London Overseas Mail Office, Stephenson Street E16 4SB, [476 6988, ext. 532].

Mount Pleasant is chiefly concerned with inland letters. Visits lasting about 90 minutes cover the mechanised sorting office and the underground railway. Because of vast quantities of mail, it's closed for visits mid-November–mid-January, for 2 weeks in April and all Bank Holidays. Otherwise it's open Monday–Thursday at 10.30, 14.30 and 19.30. Parties should not exceed 40, and application should be made to the Postmaster Controller, Mount Pleasant Post Office, Room 414, 4th Floor, Public Office Block EC1A 1BB, [837 4272, ext. 115].

National Postal Museum's aim is to stimulate an interest in collecting stamps, particularly British postage stamps. It's usually open for class visits Monday–Thursday 10.00–16.30 and Fridays 10.00–16.00. Book well in advance by writing to the Curator, National Postal Museum, London Chief Office, King Edward Street EC1A 1LP, [432 3851].
● See also p.165.

Western Central District Office arranges organised visits lasting about 2 hours and covering the sorting offices and the underground railway. It's open throughout the year (not December) Monday–Thursday 14.00–17.00. Parties should not exceed 20 in number, and application should be made to the District Postmaster, Western Central District Office, 21–31 New Oxford Street WC1A 1AA, [405 7666].

Western District Office arranges visits lasting about 90 minutes covering the sorting offices and the underground railway. It's open throughout the year (not December) Monday–Thursday 14.00–18.00. Numbers should not exceed 20, and application should be made to the District Postmaster, Western District Office, 30–50 Rathbone Place W1P 1AA, [580 3010, ext. 219].

Public buildings

Crystal Palace has a walkabout
tour lasting about 2 hours. It
features the history of the site and
lower park, highlighting its
former 1851 attractions. The
assembly point is Crystal Palace
station, and you'll be given a
souvenir map with photographs.
Accompanied children under the
age of 5 go free. Telephone [633
1707] for further information.

Houses of Parliament *see* Historic
London

Royal Hospital, Chelsea
organises guided tours. Write to
the Adjutant well in advance.

Westminster Abbey offers guided
super tours with a verger taking
you through its 900 years of
history. You'll also see the Royal
Chapels, the College Garden and,
whenever possible, the Jerusalem
Chamber. Tours usually take
place Monday–Friday at 10.00,
11.00, 14.00 and 15.00, and if
there's enough demand, on
Saturdays at 10.00, 11.00 and
12.30. Book at the Inquiry Desk
or telephone [222 7110].
● See also p.122.

Other tours

Places you can visit on your own
or in organised groups can be
found under Cricket, Football,
Music, Railways, Science and
technology, Tennis and Theatre.

Handicapped

Listed below are some of the
places accessible or partly
accessible to those in wheelchairs,
but usually only if accompanied
by an able-bodied adult.

VH: facilities for the visually
handicapped.
D: facilities for the deaf, usually
an induction loop for hearing
aids.
A: where possible, an attendant
will be on hand to help, so ring in
advance.
T: you must telephone in
advance; in fact, it would be
sensible to do so anyway since in
many places the number of
disabled that can be
accommodated is limited.

Places to visit

**All Hallows Barking-by-the-
Tower:** (11 steps to crypt; A; T).
● See also p.40.

Barbican Centre: (auditorium and
foyers accessible; D in stalls of
Barbican Theatre, seats with
amplification equipment in
Barbican Hall and Cinema I;
pamphlet with details from
information desks and box office).
● See also p.101.

Battersea Arts Centre: (mainly
accessible; D in theatre; T).
● See also p.179.

**Bear Gardens Museum and Arts
Centre**: (1 step; partly accessible;
A).
● See also p.172.

**Bethnal Green Museum of
Childhood:** (partly accessible; A;
T).
● See also p.92.

British Crafts Centre: (1 step; T.
● See also p.44.

British Museum: (wheelchairs
available; VH; A; T).
● See also p.56.

Burlington House: (A; T).
● See also p.47.

Commonwealth Institute:
(mainly accessible; VH; D; A; T).
● See also p.88.

**Courtauld Institute
Galleries:** (4 steps; A; T).
● See also p.45.

Crafts Council Gallery:
(7 steps; A).
● See also p.45.

Cutty Sark: (partly accessible).
● See also p.54.

Dulwich Picture Gallery: (A; T).
● See also p.46.

Eltham Palace: (2 steps; T).
● See also p.144.

Geffrye Museum: (A; T).
● See also p.160.

Geological Museum: (wheelchairs
available; A; T).
● See also p.112

Grange Museum: (partly
accessible; T).
● See also p.160.

Guildhall: (T).
● See also p.120.

Ham House: (9 steps; partly
accessible).
● See also p.141.

Hayward Gallery: (A).
● See also p.46.

**Heathrow Spectators' Roof
Garden:** (T).
● See also p.176.

Hogarth's House: (4 steps, partly
accessible).
● See also p.95.

Horniman Museum: (VH; A; T).
● See also p.106.

Houses of Parliament:
(Stranger's Gallery only by prior
arrangement with MP; T).
● See also p.121.

Imperial Collection: (T).
● See also p.129.

Imperial War Museum: (A; T).
● See also p.42.

IBA Broadcasting Gallery: (A;
T).
● See also p.156.

Jason's Trip: (T).
● See also p.53.

Jewel Tower: (partly accessible).
● See also p.121.

Jewish Museum: (T).
● See also p.121.

Kenwood House: (partly accessible; A; T).
● See also p.46.

Kew Bridge Engines Trust: (partly accessible; A; T).
● See also p.127.

Kodak Museum: (D; A; T).
● See also p.149.

Little Angel Marionette Theatre: (1 step; D; A; T).
● See also p.152.

London Dungeon: (A).
● See also p.107.

London Toy and Model Museum: (partly accessible; T).
● See also p.134.

London Transport Museum: (VH; A; T).
● See also p.66.

London Zoo: (VH).
● See also p.37.

Madame Tussaud's: (entry after 16.00 in July, August).
● See also p.93.

Marble Hill House: (partly accessible; A).
● See also p.121.

Museum of London: (wheelchairs available; VH; D; T).
● See also p.40.

Museum of Mankind: (8 steps; A; T).
● See also p.70.

National Army Museum: (partly accessible).
● See also p.42.

National Gallery: (wheelchairs available; T).
● See also p.46.

National Maritime Museum: (not Queen's House; VH; T).
● See also p.55.

National Museum of Labour History: (partly accessible; T).
● See also p.161.

National Postal Museum: (A).
● See also p.165.

Natural History Museum: (A; T).
● See also p.140.

Old Royal Observatory: (8 steps; partly accessible).
● See also p.73.

Polka Children's Theatre: (A; VH).
● See also p.153.

Porta Bella Packet: (A; T).
● See also p.53.

Queen's Gallery: (6 steps; partly accessible; T).
● See also p.47.

Ranger's House: (10 steps; A).
● See also p.47.

RAF, Battle of Britain, Bomber Command Museums: (VH; A).
● See also p.33.

Royal Albert Hall: (partly accessible; VH; A; T).
● See also p.137.

Royal Exchange: (use side door; T).
● See also p.123.

Royal Mews: (T).
● See also p.76.

Royal Hospital: (9 steps).
● See also p.111.

St Bride's Church: (not the crypt).
● See also p.138.

St Clement Dane's Church: (T).
● See also p.158.

St James's, Piccadilly (brass rubbing centre; 15 steps).
● See also p.59.

St Martin-in-the-Fields Church (5 steps; T).
● See also p.138.

St Paul's Cathedral: (side entrance 5 steps; crypt by arrangement).
● See also p.123.

Science Museum: (VH; T).
● See also p.157.

Serpentine Gallery: (1 step).
● See also p.47.

Southwark Cathedral: (8 steps).
● See also p.139.

Stock Exchange: (A; T).
● See also p.109.

Syon Park: (rough ground; A; T).
● See also p.67.

Tate Gallery: (wheelchairs available; T).
● See also p.47.

Thomas Coram Foundation for Children: (T).
● See also p.47.

Tower of London: (partly accessible, not Crown Jewels; A; T).
● See also p.123.

Victoria and Albert Museum: (partly accessible; T).
● See also p.139.

Wallace Collection: (2 steps).
● See also p.48.

Westminster Abbey: (4 steps to Henry VII's Chapel, not Pyx Chamber; T).
● See also p.124.

Westminster Hall: (T).
● See also p.124.

Whitechapel Art Gallery: (T).
● See also p.48.

Wimbledon Lawn Tennis Museum: (A; T).
● See also p.168.

Zoo Waterbus: (T).
● See also p.54.

Organisations

Artsline offers advice and information about London art venues. Telephone [625 5666] Tuesday–Friday 12.00–16.00, Saturday 10.00–14.00.

British Waterways Board provides details of ramps at access points and along sections of the towpath of London canals. Telephone [Watford 31363] for details.

Calibre, Aylesbury, Buckinghamshire HP20 1HU, [0296 32339] provides talking books for the blind. There's a wide selection of tapes – enough to keep a child going for quite a long time. When applying, enclose a doctor's certificate certifying inability to read printed books.

Friends for the Young Deaf, East Court Mansion, College Lane, East Grinstead, West Sussex RH19 3LT, [0342 2344] runs a Communication Through Sport project which encourages the young deaf to realise their potential in sport. There are day seminars, sports holiday courses and coaching weekends with activities ranging from archery to windsurfing. It also runs camping and drama weekends, trips to places both in and outside London, and visits abroad.

Handicapped Adventure Playground Association, Fulham Place SW6, [736 4443] has specially designed playgrounds for handicapped children. They are in use in term time, but they may be used on Saturdays and in the holidays by other handicapped children and their brothers and sisters. The association also runs a youth club and organises camping trips and holiday play schemes. The playgrounds are at:

Charlie Chaplin Playground, Bolton Crescent, Kennington Park SE5, [735 1819]
Chelsea Playground (occupies a temporary site in Battersea Park), [223 5678]
Lady Allen Playground, Chivalry Road, Wandsworth Common SW11, [228 0278]
Palace Playground, Fulham Palace, Bishops Avenue SW6, [731 2753]
Sound Playground, Weavers Field, Bethnal Green E2 has been built by professional musicians with the help of volunteers and has been constructed from recycled materials. It has resulted in sound sculpture, a kind of musical instrument where the young can develop skills in music, dance and simple instrument making, abilities they had previously not been thought capable of.

National Anglers' Council, Committee for Disabled Anglers, 11 Cowgate, Peterborough PE1 1LZ, [Peterborough 54084] for information about angling.

Riding for the Disabled, c/o British Equestrian Centre, Stoneleigh, Kenilworth, Warwickshire [Coventry 26107] for information about riding in London.

SHAPE Ticket Scheme, 9 Fitzroy Square W1T 6AE, [387 0389] for information about subsidised theatre tickets for people with various kinds of disabilities.

Thames Water, Nugent House, Vastern Road, Reading RG1 8DB; telephone Information Office [0734 593538] for information about angling and bird watching. (Four free pamphlets but send s.a.e.).

Toy Libraries Association, Seabrook House, Daikes Lane, Potters Bar, Herts [0707 44571] lends toys to handicapped children and recommends thopse to buy.

Water Sports Division of the British Sports Association for the Disabled, 29 Ironlatch Avenue, St Leonards on Sea, East Sussex TN38 9JE; telephone [Hastings 427931] daily 14.00–17.00 for advice on all water-based recreational activities in the Thames area.

Special concessions

Barbican Art Gallery has reduced admission for registered disabled.
● See also p.101.

Buckingham Palace permits parties of children in wheelchairs (not more than 50) to watch the Changing of the Guard from the forecourt. Apply well in advance to the Master of the Household with details of proposed date and number of party.
● See also p.144.

Cutty Sark is free for those in wheelchairs.
● See also p.54.

London Dungeon is free for those in wheelchairs and their pushers.
● See also p.107.

London Transport Museum is free for those in wheelchairs.
● See also p.66.

Thames Water offers concessionary rod licences and half-rate concessions on most types of fishing permits.
● See also p.115.

Sports and holiday activities

Angela Searle Playscheme is for children, and their families, who either go to school in Waltham Forest or live there, and it offers indoor and outdoor activities, trips and outings. It's open Monday–Friday 10.00–17.00 in the holidays. Go to the centre at Chase Park Lane, [524 4781] or ring [521 7111, ext. 8].

British Sports Association for the Disabled, Plumstead Baths, High Street SE18 [854 9217] has information about sports facilities in the borough.

Camden Gateway Club has swimming sessions for the mentally handicapped at Swiss Cottage Baths on Saturdays 17.30–18.30, and arranges riding at Kentish Town City Farm.

Cheyne Holiday Club for Physically Handicapped Children aged 7–16 meets at the Lady Allen Adventure Playground in the holidays (*see* Handicapped Adventure Playground Association above).

Deptford Mission to the Physically Handicapped has a junior club that meets on Mondays 18.30–20.30 at Deptford Methodist Mission, Creek Road SE8, [692 5599].

Dobbs Weir in Leaside Valley Park has special provisions for disabled anglers.

Enfield Sports Association for the Disabled, Secretary, 16 Park Avenue, Bush Hill Park, Enfield has information about local activities.

Fleetwell Swimming Club, Kentish Town Baths, Prince of Wales Road NW5 has a weekly session in the training pool for babies and children with any physical disability.

Fulham Pools have been planned so that the disabled can make use of the excellent facilities. The Duty Officer will help with personal needs.
● See also p.166.

Hammersmith and Fulham Action Sports Team has regular sessions in a whole range of sports for the mentally and physically handicapped [748 3020, ext. 293].

Haringey Hornets and London Hawks, [800 9559] organises wheelchair basketball teams. Ring for information about minimum age.

Hounslow has summer activities for the disabled, including swimming, games, outings and story times. Telephone [570 7728, ext. 3355] for information.

Hounslow's Disabled Sports and Social Club's activities include chess, wheelchair slalom, multi-gym and fitness training. It's open to those over the age of 11 and meets on the 2nd Sunday of each month in Chiswick Sports Hall.

Islington Boat Club is ready to help handicapped groups, but visits must be arranged well in advance.
● See also p.64.

Leaside Youth Centre has qualified staff to help the disabled in canoeing, sailing and rowing.
● See also p.64.

Michael Sobell Sports Centre doesn't charge the disabled for admission, but check on necessity to become a member.
● See also p.163.

Queen Mother Reservoir has dinghy and trimaran sailing for the disabled. Details from Jack Brown, 24 Boulters Court, Maidenhead, Berkshire, [Maidenhead 74715].

Richmond Asthma Swimming Group meets at the Richmond Pool on Mondays 18.30–19.00.

River Thames has two angling stations and a bench seat for the disabled upstream of Penton Lock, Staines.

Starfish Social and Swimming Club for the Disabled has classes for those with any sort of disability and of any age at Swiss Cottage Baths on Tuesdays 19.00–21.00.

Tower Hamlets Sports Association for the Disabled meets at the George Green Sports Centre for archery, bowls, table tennis and other activities; its Action Sports Team runs swimming sessions for the mentally handicapped, [247 1286].

Walthamstow Reservoirs have facilities for disabled anglers. Get in touch with Thames Water (*see* Organisations above).

Nature trails

Church Wood, Cockfosters Station: woodland trail for the blind with a continuous log trail on the ground and information points with messages in braille.

Trent Park, Enfield: nature trail for the blind; contact Parks Manager in advance, [499 8706].

Youth organisations

Scouts' policy is to integrate handicapped boys into local groups, but those wanting to join must be able to understand the Promise and the Law. Contact Mrs J. D. Bawden, 38 Perran Road SW2 3DL [674 5581].

Sea Cadet Association, Broadway House, The Broadway SW19, [540 8222] teaches skills connected with the sea and waterways. When possible, the disabled young are welcome.

Southwark's Brownies, Guides and Rangers cater for both physically and mentally handicapped girls. Contact the County Advisor, 39 Stephens Gardens, Barnhurst, Bexleyheath, Kent [252 7885].

Travel

For detailed enquiries regarding facilities for disabled passengers on London Transport, telephone the Public Relations Office, [222 5600]. London Transport also publishes *Access to the Underground*, a very detailed guide for the disabled and elderly.

Help

Emergencies

Dial 999 from any phone box (no money needed), and ask for fire, police or ambulance. You will be asked who you are, where you are speaking from and what the emergency is, and you will probably be asked to repeat the information. Don't get into a panic about it. It only takes an extra minute or two, and in the long run, it actually speeds things up.

Lost

If you are lost or have lost the person you are with, go straight to the police. If you are in a public building, go to the information desk, box office or an official for help.

Lost something

BR (all regions but Southern): property is held at the station where it was handed in. After about a week, it's forwarded to Central Lost Property, Marylebone Station, Marylebone Road NW1, [387 9400].

For Southern Region apply to local railway station or main line terminus. After a short time, lost property is forwarded to Central Lost Property above.

London Transport: call in person or write to London Transport Lost Property Office, 200 Baker Street W1. The office is open Monday–Friday 9.30–17.30, but is closed on Bank Holidays.

Taxis: call or write to 15 Penton Street NW1, or apply to nearest police station.

Chemists (all night)

H D Bliss, 50 Willesden Lane NW6, [624 8000]

Boots, Piccadilly Circus W1, [930 4761]

Dentists (emergency treatment)

Eastman Dental Hospital, 256 Grays Inn Road WC1, [838 7521] Saturday 9.00–11.00

Royal Dental Hospital, 32 Leicester Square WC2, [930 8831] 9.00–10.30, 13.30–15.00

Hospitals (24-hour casualty departments)

Guy's Hospital, St Thomas's Street SE1, [407 7600]

Hospital for Sick Children, Great Ormond Street WC1, [405 9200]

Middlesex Hospital, Mortimer Street W1, [636 8333]

New Charing Cross Hospital, Fulham Palace Road W6, [748 2040]

Royal Free Hospital, Pond Street NW3, [794 0500]

St Bartholomew's Hospital, West Smithfield EC1, [600 9000]

University College Hospital, Gower Street WC1, [387 9300]

Historic London

If you enjoy looking at historic buildings, then you should take advantage of the bargain of the year. It's a season ticket issued by the Department of the Environment, AMHB/P Store, Room 32, Building 1, Vision Way, Victoria Road, South Ruislip, Middlesex, [845 7788, ext. 259]. With this ticket, you can hurtle in and out of places in London and elsewhere, as long as the DOE looks after them. You also get a booklet listing buildings you can go in as often as you like.

London's DOE buildings include the Banqueting Hall, Chiswick House, Hampton Court, Kew Palace (not the gardens, but they're dirt cheap anyway), the Tower of London (not the Crown Jewels), and Westminster Abbey Chapter House.

Places to visit

Admiralty Arch, designed by Sir John Webb as part of the national memorial to Queen Victoria, is a triple-span entrance to the Mall from Trafalgar Square.

Bank of England is vast, covering 4 acres in all. It is known as the Old Lady of Threadneedle Street.

Look up and see why.

Banqueting Hall, designed by
Inigo Jones, was part of Whitehall
Palace. It is 110 feet long and 55
feet high, and the allegorical
paintings were designed by
Rubens. It was from here that
Charles I stepped through a
window to his execution.

Burlington Arcade, built in 1819,
has its original shop fronts. If you
are thinking of shouting,
whistling or screaming, don't.
There are beadles whose job it is
to see that nothing of the sort
takes places.

Canonbury Tower, built in 1530,
is all that's left of a marvellous
Tudor house. Down its staircase
swept people like Queen Elizabeth
I and Sir Walter Raleigh. It can
only be viewed by appointment.

Chiswick House is a beautiful
Palladian villa, built by the Earl of
Burlington in 1725. It has
splendid interiors and lovely
gardens.
● See also p.160.

Crewe House, in Mayfair, looks as
if it had strayed in from the
country. Although there's bustle
all round it, it manages to look
remarkably serene.

Crosby Hall is a building
incorporating the 15th-century
Great Hall of the original Crosby
Hall in Bishopsgate, and was

occupied by Richard III for a
short time. The Great Hall was
moved to its present site in 1910.
The effigies of Sir John Crosby,
who built it, and of his wife, can be
seen in St Helen's Church,
Bishopsgate.

Downing Street, off Whitehall, is
where the Prime Minister lives.
No 10 was given to Robert
Walpole by George II in 1731, but
instead of keeping it for himself,
Walpole decided that it should
become the official residence of
the Prime Minister.

Forty Hall, built in 1629 for a
Lord Mayor of London, is now a
small museum standing in a lovely
park with a lake.

George Inn is the last remaining
galleried inn in London. In fact,
from the courtyard you can see
the double row of galleries. At one
time they went right round the
courtyard, and were the only
means of reaching the bedrooms.
After a fire in 1677, part of the
inn was rebuilt.

Goodwin's Court is lovely. It's a
small undisturbed row of 17th-
century houses with bow windows.

Guildhall has been the City's civic
centre for centuries. In spite of
having been destroyed twice, part
of the original walls still stand.
   High over the porch are the
City's coat of arms, and from the
porch one enters the Great Hall
with stained glass windows
incorporating the names of the
664 Mayors and Lord Mayors.
The carved figures of Gog and
Magog, legendary giants, stand on

either side of the musicians' gallery. Hanging from the walls are the embroidered banners of the 12 great companies of the City.

The Guildhall is used for splendid occasions like banquets and receptions, but at times it has been used for trials like that of young Lady Jane Grey, the unfortunate queen of nine days. (Nearby cafés, restaurants.)

Henry VIII's Wine Cellar was built by Cardinal Wolsey, and was part of the original Whitehall Palace. Entry is by application to the Property Services Agency, Room 10–16, St Christopher's House, Southwark Street SE1.

House of St Barnabas, on the corner of Greek Street and Soho Square, is a typical early Georgian house. It has carved woodwork, decorative plasterwork, and a mid-Victorian French Gothic Chapel.

Houses of Parliament are built on what had been part of the site of the old royal palace of Westminster. After Henry VIII moved just up the road to Whitehall Palace, the old one was used by Parliament until it was burned down in 1834.

Work started on a new building immediately, and it was opened in 1852.

The Palace of Westminster has 100 staircases, 2 miles of passages, 11 courtyards, and over 1000 rooms, and the Victoria Tower is 336 feet high.

You can always tell when Parliament is sitting because the Union Jack will be flying and there will be a light over Big Ben.

Jewel Tower dates from 1385 and is just behind Westminster Abbey. It's one of the surviving parts of the old palace, and really was where the monarch kept his money and his jewels. It's surrounded by a very small moat where fish laze, and the building contains a small collection of objects found in and around the Houses of Parliament.

Jewish Museum has an interesting collection of Jewish antiquities, some of them very beautiful, illustrating Jewish life and faith.

Marble Hill House is a lovely Palladian building in Twickenham, built 1724–29 for the Countess of Suffolk. It houses a permanent collection of paintings and furniture. (Snacks March–October, picnic in grounds.)

Marlborough House, built by Sir Christopher Wren, once a royal residence, is now a Common-wealth Centre. Applications for conducted tours should be made to the Administration Officer.

Old Curiosity Shop was built about 1567. Although lots of people think that this was the shop that Charles Dickens wrote about, it doesn't seem very likely. Almost certainly, it started life as a dairy, when it was surrounded by green fields.

Old Palace Yard, near Westminster Hall, is the place where Guy Fawkes and his fellow conspirators were hung, drawn and quartered.
● See also p.96.

Prince Henry's Room, in Fleet Street, is believed to have been the Council Chamber of the Duchy of Cornwall in the time of James I. The room dates back to 1610, and the plaster ceiling and oak panelling are typical of the time.

Queen Anne's Gate is an elegant street with beautiful houses. Have a look at the fanlights, doorways and canopies. They really are lovely.

Queen's Chapel of the Savoy is a tiny building, and at one time was the chapel of the magnificent Savoy Palace, built by the Duke of Lancaster, and destroyed during the Peasants' Revolt in 1381. The reigning monarch is also the Duke of Lancaster, and that is why when the national anthem is sung, the first two lines are:

God save our gracious Queen,
Long live our noble Duke . . .

Roman Bath is a bit of a mystery. For a long time, it was thought to date back to Roman times, but now that's thought unlikely. Really, nobody knows who built it or why it's there. Alas, you can no longer visit it. You can only peer at it from outside.

Royal Exchange was first built 1566–68, but it was destroyed in the Great Fire. The present building was erected in 1824, and has a broad flight of stairs from which a new sovereign is proclaimed.

Royal Naval College is truly breathtaking. Opened in 1762, it was first used as a royal hospital for seamen, and later became a college for officers of the Royal Navy. The Painted Hall was designed by Sir Christopher Wren. The chapel was destroyed by fire and rebuilt in 1779, and much of the superb carving in it was carried out in the old naval dockyards in Deptford. The organ is one of the finest in the country.

Royal Opera Arcade was built by John Nash in 1816. If you've got an eye for detail, look at the bow-fronted Regency shops, the lovely lamps and glass-domed vaults.

St John's Gate is a surprise. It's all that's left of the Priory of the Order of the Knights Hospitallers of St John. The rooms over the gateway house the museum.
● See also p.42.

St Paul's Cathedral stands at the top of Ludgate Hill, and was built on the site of Old St Paul's, destroyed during the Great Fire. Built of Portland stone, and designed by Sir Christopher Wren, it is 515 feet long and 180 feet wide across the west front. The dome is 112 feet in diameter, and its height from the floor to the top of the cross is 363 feet. See if you can spot a phoenix – it symbolises the new St Paul's rising from the ashes of the old. (Cafés, restaurants nearby).

◈ 🏛 ♿ (not Crypt, Whispering Gallery, Stone Gallery, Golden Gallery)

Temple Bar was built in 1670 to mark one of the boundaries of the City of London, but later it was moved to Theobald's Park. The present memorial was erected in 1880, and it is at this point that the Lord Mayor surrenders his sword to the Queen when she enters the City of London.

Tower Wharf has a battery of guns, which are fired on special occasions. Each gun bears a tablet telling you all about it.

Tower of London, built by William the Conqueror but extended by other kings, was meant to over awe Londoners, and was regarded with dread. It has had many functions, and has served as a fortress, a royal residence, a prison, the mint, an observatory and even as a menagerie, many of them at the same time.

The oldest building is the White Tower, and it stands on the spot where the Romans chose to build a fortress. William II, obviously not thinking it strong enough, began constructing an inner wall, building thirteen protective towers, and other kings added yet more fortifications.

One of the best known towers is the Bloody Tower, and it's there that the young princes, children of Edward IV, were last seen alive. The mystery of their death has never been solved, and historians still argue over whether the bones buried at the foot of the tower were theirs or not. It was in this tower that Sir Walter Raleigh and many other famous people were imprisoned.

Beauchamp Tower, like the others, has inscriptions painfully scratched on its walls by prisoners. One refers to Lady Jane Grey, the nine-day queen. Mary Tudor soon put an end to her reign, and the girl was imprisoned. From this tower, she saw her husband taken to his execution, and saw his body carried back, while she was awaiting her own death.

Tower Hill, where the ravens hop about, was the site of many executions. An enclosure marks the spot where the scaffold was erected for the execution of people of importance.

If you want to see how the Tower of London developed, look at the History Gallery, which shows with the aid of models just how it grew.

The Crown Jewels are kept in the Jewel House. Most of the regalia isn't very old, for after the death of Charles I, much of it was sold off or melted down. But in spite of that, it's a stunning display. (Refreshments on Tower Wharf, picnic area.)

Trafalgar Square was laid out to commemorate Nelson's victory at the battle of Trafalgar, but it was not until 1852 that it was completed. It's reported that 14 people actually dined on the top of the column before Nelson's statue was placed in position.

London Experience in the **Trocadero** offers a 40-minute journey through time with the help of five screens and lots of projectors. The show is well-named. It really is an experience. Screenings start at about 10.00 and go on until 22.00.

Wardrobe Place, off Carter Lane, is a charming square with 17th- and 18th-century houses. It got its name because it was here that the King's Wardrobe, actually a warehouse stuffed with furniture and armoury, was kept.

Westminster Abbey was originally a Benedictine Abbey. The abbey church was built by Edward the Confessor, and consecrated in 1065, and he was buried in front of the altar. William the Conqueror decided that this was the place where he was going to be crowned, and every monarch has followed suit. Henry III pulled down much of the original church, and built other bits, and Henry VII built the beautiful

chapel named after him. The final alteration was made in 1739, when Hawksmoor designed the western towers.

There is a great deal to see – the tomb of the Unknown Soldier, Poet's Corner, St George's Chapel, dedicated to those who died in the First World War, the Chapel of St John the Baptist with its 15th-century tombs and the Chapel of St Edward the Confessor. You'll probably be a bit disappointed by the Coronation Chair, an oak chair made for Edward I, since it certainly doesn't look grand. Beneath it is the Stone of Scone, the coronation seat of the kings of Scotland, which Edward I took as part of his booty in 1297. (*See* Houses of Parliament).

   (not Coronation Chair, royal tombs)

Westminster Hall was built by William II as part of the Palace of Westminster, and is the largest hall in Europe with its roof unsupported by pillars. It's 238 feet long, 90 feet high, and over 67 feet wide. The niches and window recesses in the south and east walls hold 14th-century statues of kings.

Westminster Hall has been used as the chief law courts and for important trials like that of Charles I and of Guy Fawkes and his fellow conspirators.

Ice skating

Although you might not be very good at it, ice skating is fun, even if you do keep falling over. However, if you'd rather stay upright, you could take lessons at any of the rinks mentioned below.

Organisation

National Skating Association, 15 Gee Street EC1, [253 3824] is the governing body of this sport and it provides information and advice.

Ice rinks

All the following rinks have skates for hire.

Lee Valley Ice Centre is London's newest rink with a full-size ice pad and seating for about 1000 spectators. There's group and individual tuition available, and those keen on ice hockey and curling are also catered for. It's open 7 days a week with 3 sessions a day Friday–Wednesday, and 2 on Thursdays, but times vary, so ring for details.

Michael Sobell Sports Centre has 3 sessions a day, but there's no skating on weekday mornings in term time. There's a family session on Sundays 15.00–17.00, and Monday evenings 19.00–21.00 are for under 14s only. At the moment skating is free for the unemployed, but check to make sure that the policy hasn't changed.
● See also p.163.

Queen's Ice Club is open daily with 3 sessions a day, and there are children's classes after school on Thursdays and Fridays.

Richmond Ice Drome is open 7 days a week with 3 sessions a day, and you can have private tuition or join children's classes.

Streatham Ice Rink has 3 sessions a day each day of the week, and has special children's classes.

Industrial archaeology

(*see also* Bridges and tunnels)

People have become more aware of the importance of industrial archaeology during the last few years. This is the study, recording and preservation of industrial buildings like mines, factories and mills and of the machinery that worked them.

There's so much to see in London that we've listed just a few places to give you some idea of what it's all about.

Places to visit

Bromley-by-Bow has a tidemill – a kind of water mill. Once there were three mills, but only two remain. The Clock Mill has been carefully restored, but it is used as offices. However, you can see the wheels from a special viewing platform. The House Mill will be restored some time in the future. Group visits of not more than 20 can be arranged by contacting Messrs Hedges and Butler Ltd, Three Mills Lane E3, [980 7133].

Brixton Mill is a tower mill erected in 1816. It fell into disuse, was rescued by the GLC, and provided with machinery from a derelict mill in Lincolnshire.

Fulham Gasometer, built in 1830 with a capacity of 250,000 cubic feet of gas, is the oldest gas holder in the world.

Kingsbury Water Mill has three grinding stones, all driven by water. It ground corn up to 1960, but then was no longer needed. In 1970 it was restored, and it is now in working order.

New King's Road had a pottery at one time. You can see the 19th-century bottle kiln revealed in 1975.

St Pancras Station, built 1867–74, is a marvellous example of Victorian Gothic architecture. The vault over the train hall is nearly 700 feet long and almost 205 feet wide. When built, it was the greatest covered area in the world.

Spitalfields used to be the heart of the silk-weaving industry in London, an area in which Huguenot refugees settled. If you walk along Fournier Street and Wilkes Street, you'll see houses built 1720–30. At the very top of some of the houses are extremely tall windows so that the weavers could get the maximum light in which to do their work.

Surrey Iron Railway was the first public railway in the world – not that it had trains. There was a double track with rails on stone sleepers so that horses could pull wagons along. Parts of the railway can be seen in the grounds of Wallington Public Library.

Truman's Brewery in Brick Lane stands on a site where beer has been brewed for centuries. Some of the buildings are 18th-century warehouses.

Upminster has a splendid smock mill, and there's an excellent model of it in the reference department of Romford Library.

Wimbledon Windmill Museum uses models, pictures, machinery and tools to illustrate the history of windmills.

Museums

Kew Bridge Engines Trust has impressive beam engines dating from 1820, the largest of their kind in the world, and you can see some of them in full steam. There's also a working forge, traction engines and models, and the trust is establishing a unique museum showing the development of London's water supply.

Museum of London has a lot of surprising exhibits, including the original screens and lift interior from Selfridge's.
● See also p.40.

National Maritime Museum has many examples of industrial archaeology, including the riveted steam paddle tug *Reliant*. You can see its unique side-lever engines in motion. There's also a steam launch *Waterlily* and a set of early marine and diesel and petrol engines.
● See also p.55.

Science Museum has so much on show that it's hard to know what to include. However, don't miss the early beam engines, steam boilers and turbines, hot air gas and oil engines, and the display showing the development of motive power. There's glass technology, the history of iron and steel, and items on the development of agricultural and textile machinery.
● See also p.157.

Tower Bridge Museum traces the history of the bridge, the Thames and other London bridges back to 1176. You can see the control room and the massive Victorian engines which raised the bascules, one of them still in working order. There's a display with models, pictures, diagrams and a short video film.
● See also p.61.

Vestry House Museum is housed in an early 18th-century workhouse and contains material connected with the locality. What is more, it's the home of what is said to be Britain's first motor car.

Whitehall, a timber-framed house built about 1500, is fascinating. Features reveal sections of the original fabric, and displays include the medieval pottery. (Refreshments.)

Information

Children's London is a recorded, chatty telephone service giving details of the week's events, [246 8007].

City of London Information Centre St Paul's Churchyard EC4, [606 3030] offers advice and information about the square mile. It has some free literature, and it's always well worth picking up its monthly diary of events.

Clerkenwell Heritage/Urban Studies Centre 33 St John's Square EC1 [250 1039], is open April–September Monday–Friday 9.00–18.00, Saturday, Sunday 14.00–17.00; October–March Monday–Friday 10.00–17.00 has information about local events, places of historic interest, craft centres and museums.

Croydon Tourist Information Centre Katharine Street, Croydon, Surrey [688 3627 ext 45/46], is open Monday 9.30–19.00, Tuesday–Friday 9.30–18.00, Saturday 9.00–17.00 has information about annual and special events, music, drama, clubs and so on.

Daily Telegraph Information Bureau supplies general information Monday–Friday 9.30–17.30, [353 4242].

Greenwich Tourist Information Centre Cutty Sark Gardens SE10 [858 6376] is open April–October daily 10.30–17.30; November–March Saturday, Sunday 11.00–17.00 has up-to-date information about historic Greenwich and local events.

Guildhall Library has historical information about the city of London.
● See also p.120.

Kidsline, Capital Radio's information service, will let you know what's on where, suggests holiday schemes, and even new hobbies. It operates 16.00–18.00 on weekdays during term time, and 9.00–16.00 during the holidays, [222 8070].

Kingston-upon-Thames Tourist Information Centre Heritage Centre, Fairfield West, Kingston-upon-Thames, Surrey [546 5386], is open Monday–Saturday 10.00–17.00 for information about places of interest, annual and special events, clubs, etc.

Hillingdon Tourist Information Centre 22 High Street, Uxbridge, Middlesex [0895 5076] is open Monday–Friday 9.30–20.00, Saturday 9.30–17.00 will let you know about activities and events in the locality.

Lewisham Tourist Information Centre Borough Mall, Lewisham Centre SE13 [318 5421/2] is open Monday–Friday 9.15–17.15 for information about all local activities and places of interest.

London Visitor and Convention Bureau's Tourist Information Centre Victoria Station Forecourt SW1 (telephone information service [730 3488] Monday–Friday 9.00–17.30) is open daily 9.00–20.30 with extended hours in July, August.

Jewellery

London Transport Information
Centres are at Euston, Heathrow
Central, King's Cross, Oxford
Circus, Piccadilly Circus, Victoria
and St James's Park tube stations.
They deal with enquiries about
buses, tubes, and Green Line
coaches, and provide free bus and
underground maps and leaflets.
St James's Park is closed on
Saturdays, Sundays and public
holidays; Oxford Circus is closed
on Sundays. There is a 24-hour
telephone service, [222 1234].

Lordship Lane Information
Centre 25 Lordship Lane SE22,
[693 0618] has details of all
organisations and activities in
Southwark.

Richmond-upon-Thames Tourist
Information Centre Richmond
Central Library, Little Green,
Richmond [940 9125] is open
Monday, Thursday, Friday
10.00–18.00, Tuesday, Saturday
10.00–17.00, Wednesday 10.00–
20.00 and has information about
all local events, places of historic
interest, museums and activities in
the borough.

Tower Hamlets Tourist
Information Centre 88 Roman
Road E2 [980 3749] open
Monday–Friday 9.00–17.30, has
information about everything
that's going on in the borough.

Twickenham Tourist
Information Centre District
Library, Garfield Road,
Twickenham, Middlesex [892
0032] is open Monday, Thursday,
Friday 10.00–18.00, Tuesday,
Wednesday, Saturday 10.00–
17.00 has information about local
events, clubs and places of interest
in the locality.

Although few of us are likely to
own valuable jewellery, it's lovely
to look at, and the more you look,
the more you'll learn – after all,
you never know. You might be
lucky. Secondhand jewellery is
usually a good buy, so look round
the markets. Try Camden Lock,
Camden Passage, Cutler Street,
Jubilee, the New Caledonian and
Portobello Road markets.

Places to visit

British Museum has all sorts of
jewellery. Some of the most
spectacular comes from the
Sutton Hoo burial ship and
includes a stunning silver face
mask and gold and garnet
jewellery.
● See also p.56.

Geological Museum has a world-
famous collection of gemstones,
all beautifully displayed. There
are replicas of famous stones like
the Koh-i-Noor, and a display
explains the use of industrial
diamonds.
● See also p.129.

Imperial Collection has 180
marvellous replicas of crowns,
swords, coronation regalia,
necklaces, and so on, all made by
master craftsmen. The effect is
dazzling. Among the exhibits is

the Imperial Crown of the Tsars, studded with 4936 diamonds, the ruby and diamond tiara of the Queen of Bavaria, and the glittering coronation crown of the Empress Farah Diba. The Crown of the Andes is fascinating. Originally it was made from a solid block of gold in 1596.

Museum of London has examples of jewellery from many ages. In its Tudor section is the Cheapside Hoard. This is thought to be the stock of a 16th-century jeweller who hid it beneath the floor of his shop during one of the many outbreaks of plague in the early 17th century. You'll see necklaces, hair ornaments, brooches and earrings.
● See also p.40.

Tower of London, as everyone knows, holds the Crown Jewels. Most of the early regalia was sold or melted down during the Commonwealth although some was recovered at the Restoration, but it means that most was made after 1660. However, in the Imperial State Crown, which is made of gold and has 3000 diamonds in it, there's the huge uncut ruby given to the Black Prince in 1367.
● See also p.123.

Victoria and Albert Museum has a sparkling jewellery gallery.
● See also p.139.

Law

The area around Chancery Lane is the legal centre of London. Here you will find the four Inns of Court where lawyers have had their offices, known as chambers, since the reign of Edward I in the 13th century. Chancery Lane itself has stationers, patent agents and others occupied with the law, as well as the Law Society.

Inns of Court

Gray's Inn is entered through a 17th-century gateway in High Holborn, and you can walk in the gardens and watch barristers playing croquet in the summer. The oldest of the catalpa trees is said to have been grown from a cutting brought from America by Sir Walter Raleigh.

The Hall was built 1556–60, was destroyed during the Second World War, and has been rebuilt in its original style. You can see the Hall on application to the Under-Treasurer.

Lincoln's Inn can be reached through an archway at the south-east corner of Lincoln's Inn Fields, although the main entrance is in Chancery Lane. There's a beautiful chapel with an open crypt, and you can wander in this and in the precincts. The 15th-century hall is well worth a visit with its heraldic glass and vast mural painted by Watts. Apply at the gatehouse for admission Monday–Friday.

The Temple consists of two Inns of Court, Middle Temple and Inner Temple. It was originally the property of the Knights Templar, crusaders founded in Jerusalem in the early 12th century. Later, they were turned out, and lawyers began to move in. You can reach the Temple through a 17th-century gateway in Fleet Street.

Middle Temple Hall, opened by Elizabeth I in 1576, was badly damaged during the Second World War, but it's been marvellously restored, using original materials where possible. It has a complicated double hammerbeam roof and fine panelling, and you can still see the Elizabethan carved screen. It was here that Shakespeare's *Twelfth Night* was first performed. The serving table was made from the timbers of the *Golden Hind*, Sir Francis Drake's ship.

Inner Temple Hall was also almost completely destroyed by bombing, and has been rebuilt, but you can still see the buttery, a vaulted chamber, and the 14th-century crypt.

Temple Church serves both Inns of Court. It has a circular nave, based on the Church of the Holy Sepulchre in Jerusalem, and completed in 1185. Alas, it too was damaged, but has been very carefully restored. It was in the nave, known as the 'round', that lawyers awaited their clients.

Courts

If you'd like to see British justice in action, you can go to magistrates' courts, the Royal Courts of Justice or the Old Bailey to watch cases being brought, but you must be over the age of 14.

Old Bailey is the Central Criminal Court where all the most serious cases are tried, and it stands on the site of the old Newgate prison. The judges still carry posies of flowers at the beginning of sessions, a reminder of the old days when the stench coming from the prisons below must have been appalling. There's a large open space in front of the building, and that's where public executions used to take place. If you look up, you'll see the Lady of Justice carrying scales and a sword. If you want to see a trial, queue at the door in Newgate Street or the Public Gallery entrance.

Royal Courts of Justice, more often known as the Law Courts, houses the Court of Appeal and the Chancery, Family and Queen's Bench Divisions. The public are admitted when the court is in session.

Events (*see* Calendar)

Opening of the Law Courts

Quit Rents Ceremony

Markets

The open-air street markets of London provide some of the best, free entertainment – not to mention a few bargains. Generally speaking, they are noisy, good-humoured, and often amusing. They divide into two kinds; wholesale markets sell to the trade; retail markets to the general public.

Wholesale markets

To see these at their best, you have to be up before the crack of dawn. By mid-morning there is almost nothing to see.

New Covent Garden in Nine Elms is where the old Covent Garden fruit and vegetable market moved to in 1974. Although it hasn't got the same charm and atmosphere as the old market, there's still plenty of colourful activity.

Smithfield deals in meat, poultry and provisions and is the biggest meat market in the world, covering 10 acres and with two miles of shop frontage. Originally it was called 'Smooth Fair' and has been used for tournaments, executions and fairs. Look out for the statue of Henry VII. It is the only one in London.

Spitalfields is the Corporation of London's fruit and vegetable market, with the Flower Market and the Fruit Exchange next to it. The main market frontage is well over a mile long. This market was established in 1682, although trading was carried on long before then.

Retail markets

Berwick Street Market is in the middle of colourful Soho, and street trading has been carried on there for about 200 years. It sells fruit, vegetables, fish and poultry all mixed up with household goods.

Brixton Market is a noisy, colourful place selling practically everything you need in the house, as well as clothes, fruit and vegetables, and bric-a-brac. The most noticeable thing about the market is the strong West Indian atmosphere – reggae music pours out of nearby record shops and people sing aloud in the streets and walk in rhythm to the infectious beat.

Camden Lock Market is an art and crafts centre, and you can see the workshops where weaving, jewellery making, knitting and so on is done. There's also antiques, bric-a-brac and secondhand books. At the back of the market there's a cobbled courtyard by the canal lock where buskers play.

Camden Passage in Islington is an open antique market with shops on either side of the passage. It isn't large, but it's interesting, especially with the canal nearby.

However, you're unlikely to find a bargain as everything is rather pricey.

Chapel Market in Islington is a mixed market, with fruit, vegetables, clothes and unusual plants and it's busiest at weekends.

Columbia Road in Bethnal Green specializes in plants, flowers and gardening equipment. It's particularly busy at springtime.

Cutler Street, near Petticoat Lane, is a self-contained market of 40 stalls selling gold and jewellery. The small area is so packed with people on Sunday mornings that it's almost impossible to move.

East Street, Walworth, is a large market selling fruit and vegetables, plants, clothes, toys, general household goods and junk.

Farringdon Road Market, Clerkenwell, is a secondhand book and manuscript market. It's open during the week, but Saturday is definitely the most lively day.

Greenwich Antique Market has stalls selling coins, medals, secondhand books, jewellery and old clothes as well as antiques and bric-a-brac. It's open on Saturday mornings, but you'd need to be early to pick up a bargain.

Inverness Street Market in Camden Town has mainly fruit and vegetable stalls, but at the far end there are all sorts of junk and secondhand bargains to be had.

Jubilee Market is a small general market near the restored Covent Garden piazza. It specialises in certain goods on different days, and the art and crafts at weekends are particularly interesting. You can buy anything from stained glass to hand-knitted sweaters.

Kingsland Waste in Dalston is well-known for its secondhand bikes and spare parts. It's a market for the 'do-it-yourself' brigade – just the place to look for that vital mechanical part. You can also buy fruit and vegetables, clothes and bric-a-brac. It's at its liveliest on Saturday mornings.

Leadenhall Market was originally a wholesale poultry market, but it has become a retail one with over 70 shops selling poultry, meat, fish, game and cheese. The market is now housed in a great late-Victorian iron and glass building, but there's been a market on the site since Roman times.

Leather Lane in Holborn is a lunchtime market selling household goods and foodstuffs. The only leather you'll see is a stall selling chamois leathers.

New Caledonian Market in Bermondsey Square is the largest regular antique market in southern England. It's open only on Friday, from dawn to 13.00, but by 10.30 the place is becoming dead. Dealers buy a great deal here and you will find all sorts of things, including furniture, bric-a-brac, silver, jewellery, watches, pottery and porcelain. You'll need to be up very early to pick up a bargain.

Petticoat Lane is one of the most famous street markets in the world. People go there because of its unique atmosphere – the sheer noise, energy and activity is so typical of the East Enders. The street traders are an entertainment in themselves. The market sells just about everything.

Piccadilly Market is a fairly new art and craft market in the forecourt of St James's Church. You'll find bric-a-brac, second-hand clothes, shells and fossils, coins and stamps as well.

Portobello Road is well known for its antiques, particularly on a Saturday, when it is absolutely packed with stalls selling furniture, paintings, pottery, porcelain, old clothes and bric-a-brac. You can also buy green-grocery, and household goods – and you'll mingle with people of all races and types.

Walthamstow High Street is a huge, lively market selling practically everything, including live trout swimming around in a tank.

Wembley Market, in the stadium car park, is the largest and best-known of several Sunday markets that started about 12 years ago to make use of an open area only otherwise used during the week. There are so many stalls it's impossible to visit them all – and in any case the crowds are so great you wouldn't get near some of them. You can buy almost anything – though it's all new, not secondhand. Similar Sunday markets are held at Lea Valley Viaduct, Dagenham Dock and the Western International Sunday Market at Southall.

Westmoreland Road, Walworth, sells mainly fruit and vegetables and household goods during the week, but on Sunday mornings its character changes completely and it becomes a popular hunting ground for antiques, bric-a-brac, secondhand bikes, records and books.

Models

Any model or model-making exhibition is bound to be a success since people of all ages are fascinated by them. London's well supplied with shops selling models and model-making kits, and there are lots on display.

Places to visit

Imperial War Museum has a collection of model military ships and aircraft.
● See also p.42.

London Toy and Model Museum has now expanded into an adjoining building, so there are even more exhibits on display. There's the Tiatsa Model Car Collection (you won't be able to miss the bear driving a quarter scale Cadillac of 1916), lots of trains, including an 1845 scale model, probably used as a sample, and a working garden railway. There are occasional model locomotive trials, and one Sunday a month all are welcome with their working model trains. (Refreshments; picnic in Kensington Gardens, a bit of a walk.)

London Transport Museum has model exhibitions from time to time. Ring up or watch national newspapers for information.
● See also p.66.

National Army Museum has many models of all sorts of things. There's one of a street scene demonstrating the way the army copes with urban terrorists.
● See also p.42.

National Maritime Museum has splendid models. Two are particularly impressive. They are sections of the *Great Britain* of 1843 and the *Windsor Castle* of 1970, showing the difference in passenger accommodation. There are also some original 17th-century scale models of ships that the naval authorities were thinking of building.
● See also p.55.

Science Museum is crammed with models of all kinds, many of them working. Don't miss HMS *Prince*. It's considered by many to be the most magnificent model ever made.
● See also p.157.

Places to sail model boats

Some of the places to launch your boat are at Blackheath, Parliament Hill, the Round Pond in Kensington Gardens, Thamesmead, Victoria Park and Whitestone Pond, Hampstead. The model boating lake in Brockwell Park SE26 can be used only on Sundays.

Events (*see* Calendar)

Model Engineer Exhibition

International Model Railway Exhibition

European Festival of Model Railways

Music

There's so much going on in the music world that it is difficult to know where to begin. No matter how hard up you are, if you want to learn to play an instrument there will be a class you can join. If you just want to listen to music, then there are concerts on all the time, music in the open during the summer, and free music in London's churches.

Taking part

Battersea Arts Centre has a music workshop for parents and children, and a guitar workshop for young beginners.
● See also p.179.

Ernest Read Music Association has summer courses at Gipsy Hill. Ring for information.

Greenwich Young People's Theatre has a rock music workshop for those aged 14+ which offers an opportunity for young people to develop their individual music skills or to work in a group.
● See also p.169.

Islington Dance Factory has music sessions for 8–14 year-olds on Thursdays after school. Here you get a chance to become familiar with all kinds of instruments, and generally to

have fun with music.
● See also p.87.

London College of Music runs a Saturday junior music school for those aged 10+.

Morley College has a music workshop on Saturday mornings where the whole family can go along and play various instruments and try their hand at composing. There's plenty of action, songs and games for young children, while older ones can experiment on the electronic equipment. There's also a workshop for families with a mentally handicapped child.

Music Centre in Hounslow runs Saturday morning music workshops at four venues in the borough. There is individual tuition and group activities with a wide range of instruments, as well as choral work.

Oval House is the place for those aged 16 and over to learn how to play an instrument or join in group music making.
● See also p.179.

Tower Hamlets Youth Dance Centre has a music workshop for all ages on Saturday mornings.
● See also p.88.

Trent Park Music Centre has a Saturday Morning Music Club where kids have the opportunity of playing instruments, singing and listening to music on tape.

Young Audiences of Chiswick was started by the singer Gillian Humphreys to introduce children to the world of music and give them confidence to perform in concerts with her. The concerts raise funds for charitable causes.

Youth Music Centre in Hampstead is a Saturday morning music school for children aged 4–17 years. The youngest children can begin in an informal percussion group, then progress to the recorder, a stringed or wind instrument. There are classes and the chance to play in an ensemble or orchestra. There's a summer music and recreation course for older children.

Listening

Arthur Davidson Orchestral Concerts are a series of orchestral concerts given on Saturday mornings October–May at the Fairfield Hall, Croydon. Concerts consist of a selection of short pieces to introduce a wide variety of instruments.

Atarah's Band Fun Concerts are held in the Queen Elizabeth Hall in school holidays. These are really fun, and full of surprises. Children are encouraged to take their own instrument along.

Barbican Centre has lunchtime concerts on Wednesdays at 13.00.
● See also p.101.

Ernest Read Concerts are held in the Festival Hall on Saturday mornings, and are suitable for children over 7.

GLC puts on open-air concerts during the summer months at *Crystal Palace Park*, *Holland Park* and *Kenwood*.

Henry Wood Promenade Concerts held in the Royal Albert Hall are not specifically aimed at young people, but they are remarkably cheap if you are happy to stand or sit on the floor.

Morley College Family Concerts are designed to introduce parents and children to a wide variety of music, from classical to pop, and from ethnic to electronic. Children can participate in the excitement of listening to music and dance to it.

Queen Elizabeth Hall and Purcell Room often hold special concerts for children during the school holidays. These have included Tinderbox, Gerard and Jean, Michael and Doreen Muskett.

Robert Mayer Concerts take place on six Saturday mornings between October and March in the Royal Festival Hall. They are intended for 8–13 year-olds.

Royal Festival Hall usually has free music at lunchtimes, and in the Music Box at weekends.

Brass band concerts

GLC organises band concerts in Battersea Park, Burgess Park, Cutty Sark Gardens, Finsbury Park, Golders Hill Park, Holland Park, Horniman Gardens, Jubilee Gardens, Parliament Hill, Victoria Park.

Hyde Park: Sunday afternoon and evening performances in June and July.
● See also p.148.

Lincoln's Inn Fields: lunchtime performances from May to August.
● See also p.107.

Regent's Park: performances on Sunday afternoons and evenings during the summer.
● See also p.149.

St James's Park: daily performances during the summer.
● See also p.149.

Victoria Embankment Gardens: daily afternoon and evening performances during May, June and July.
● See also p.48.

Music in churches

Some churches have regular lunchtime concerts, and these are usually free. To check times ring the City of London Information Centre.

All Hallows Barking-by-the-Tower: Thursday 12.15, 13.15 (often organ recitals)
● See also p.40.

Bishopsgate Institute: Tuesday, Thursday 13.05 (classical and chamber music)
● See also p.56.

Holy Sepulchre: Wednesday 13.15

St Anne and St Agnes: Monday 13.10

St Bartholomew-the-Great: Thursday 13.10 (and other occasional concerts)

St Botolph Without: Thursday 13.10 (piano recital).

St Bride's: Wednesday 13.15 (organ and harp recitals).

St James's Piccadilly: Thursday 13.05.
● See also p.59.

St John's Smith Square: Monday 13.00 (usually instrumental).

St Lawrence Jewry: Tuesday 13.00 (and other occasional concerts).

St Margaret Lothbury: Wednesday 13.10.

St Martin-in-the-Fields: Monday, Tuesday 13.05 (choral and chamber music).

St Martin-within-Ludgate: Friday 13.15 (and other occasional concerts).

St Mary-le-Bow: Thursday 13.05 (recordings).
● See also p.143.

St Michael's Cornhill: Monday 13.00 (organ recitals).

St Olave's: Thursday 13.05 (classical recitals).
● See also p.95.

St Paul's Cathedral: occasional Fridays 12.30 (organ recitals).
● See also p.123.

St Peter's Cornhill: Tuesday 12.30.

St Stephen Walbrook: Friday 12.30.

Southwark Cathedral: Monday 13.10 (organ recital); Tuesday, Thursday 12.30 (recorded music).

Museums

Fenton House has a collection of musical instruments – harpsichords, virginals and spinets. The oldest is a curious five-sided spinet of 1540.
● See also p.151.

Horniman Museum's collection of musical instruments comes from all over the world. There are drums made out of logs and shell trumpets.
● See also pp.106.

Museum of Instruments in the Royal College of Music is open on Wednesdays during term time by appointment with the Curator. There are hundreds of instruments ranging from Haydn's clavichord to hurdy-gurdies. Many of them come from other countries.

Museum of London has instruments on display, and if you listen carefully at some show cases, you'll hear music of the period. In the section devoted to the late 19th century you'll see, and might even hear, a barrel organ.
● See also p.40.

Musical Museum holds an astonishing collection of about 200 instruments – cinema organs, pianos and jazz pianos, dulcimers, orchestrions, the only self-playing Wurlitzer in Europe, and so on. All the instruments play, and they are explained and demonstrated to you. Quiet is essential, so it's not a good place for young children. Send s.a.e. for details of tours.

Ranger's House in Greenwich has the wonderful Arnold Dolmetsch collection of 18th-century musical instruments.

Victoria and Albert Museum has a Musical Instruments Gallery, and there are recordings of music being played. Look out for the giraffe's piano – it's called that because it looks a bit like one. Actually, it's not just a piano. It's got drums and bells too. (Refreshments.)

Natural history

(*see also* Animals and birds,
Flowers and plants, Conservation)

It is lucky that there are so many
open spaces in London, since
anyone interested in natural
history really has an opportunity
to get out and pursue his hobby.
For the real enthusiast, museums
provide much valuable
information and data.

Places to visit

Broomfield Museum, an old
mansion in Palmer's Green, is
concerned with Southgate's rural
past, with comprehensive displays
of mammals, fish and butterflies,
mostly of local origin. There's also
a glass-fronted beehive.
(Refreshments, picnic in park.)

Epping Forest Museum is
concerned with conservation.
Display boards describe the
history and wildlife of Epping
Forest.

Greenwich Borough Museum has
a good natural history collection
specifically related to the area.

Horniman Museum has a large
natural history collection which
includes stuffed animals and birds
from every continent, fossils, an
exhibition explaining evolution,
an aquarium, and a beehive.
● See also p.106.

London Butterfly House is set in
an acre of parkland and mature
trees bordered by a lake – the
perfect setting for breeding and
studying the stages of
development of butterflies.
There's a large greenhouse
structure for tropical and
temperate species – if you're lucky
you might actually see a butterfly
emerging from its pupa. There
are also a number of other insects
and arachnids, including giant
spiders, leaf-cutting ants and
scorpions.

Natural History Museum has so
much to see it's difficult to know
where to start. Some new learn-
and-enjoy exhibitions have
opened recently: dinosaurs and
their living relatives; the hall of
human biology, introducing
ecology; man's place in evolution;
origin of species; and British
natural history. (Cafeteria, picnic
in grounds.)

Passmore Edwards Museum has
an exhibition of the natural
history of the area.

Needlework

Even if you can't manage to sew on a button, you might well find that you get a great deal of pleasure out of seeing really exquisite pieces of work.

Places to visit

Bethnal Green Museum of Childhood has examples of locally made Spitalfields silks.
● See also p.92.

Ham House has 17th-century textiles and sets of chairs upholstered in their original fabrics. There's even a toilet set made from Lyons silk with silver brocade in about 1730. Other exhibits include tapestries and carpets. (Refreshment room, April–September.)

 (partly accessible)

Hampton Court Palace has tapestries made in 1662. You'll see them in the Queen's Gallery.
● See also p.145.

National Army Museum has uniforms, richly embroidered with gold and silver braid. Even the Duke of Blenheim's saddle cloth is stiff with the stuff.
● See also p.42.

Notre Dame de France, in Leinster Place in Bayswater, has a large Aubusson tapestry.

Royal School of Needlework has heavily embroidered vestments, altar cloths and banners.

Victoria and Albert Museum has a remarkable collection of embroidered fabrics, and there's a 15th–16th century collection of tapestries.
● See also p.139.

William Morris Gallery has examples of the designs for his famous cottons and chintzes, and it possesses some beautifully embroidered silk panels.
● See also p.48.

Odds and ends

London has lots of attractive little corners, statues, and relics which don't seem to fit into any particular category, but it would be a pity not to see them if you happen to be in the vicinity.

Amen Court is a peaceful place in the City, with its 17th-century houses.

Artillery Passage is a medieval alley, with early 19th-century shop fronts. No. 56 is said to have the most beautiful shop front in England.

Bank of England had a clerk who was 6 feet 7 inches tall. When he died, there were body snatchers about, and so he was buried in the bank's Fountain Court, the safest place in the whole of the City.
• See also p.119.

Cleopatra's Needle has nothing to do with Cleopatra, but it did come from Egypt. There's an amazing collection of objects buried beneath it – Queen Victoria's portrait, a verse from St John's gospel in 215 languages, Genesis translated into Arabic, a newspaper of the day, and many other things.

Clink Street has given us the word 'clink' since it was there that the Clink Prison stood.

Duke of York's Column is in Waterloo Place. He was an extravagant man, and it was said that he was stuck up there to escape from his creditors. Perhaps it was also to escape the wrath of the army. Every soldier was stopped a day's pay to pay for it.

Eros, in Piccadilly Circus, commemorated the 7th Earl of Shaftesbury, who worked for the welfare of children.

Frances Stuart's parrot, stuffed, of course, can be seen with her effigy in Westminster Abbey Museum. She was the original model for Britannia on the old pennies.

23–24 Leinster Gardens aren't houses at all. The fronts are dummies built over the cutting for the Circle line to preserve the appearance of the street.

Liverpool Street Station is built on the site of an old plague pit.

Marble Arch was intended to be a grand new entrance for Buckingham Palace. It wasn't until it was finished that it was discovered that the arch was too narrow for the state coach to pass through.

Panier Alley has a relief of a boy seated on a pannier on steps leading to the alley. A little rhyme claims that it's the highest point of the City – it isn't.

Postman's Park is in the churchyard of St Botolph's Without. There are art nouveau tiles recording acts of bravery in Victorian times.

Quadriga, at the top of Constitution Hill, was sculpted by Captain Adrian John. It took four years to complete, and when it was finished, he gave a tea-party inside the horses.

St Mary-le-Bow has Bow Bells. Unless you're born within the sound of them, you can't call yourself a cockney.

Vintner's Hall is where five cheers are given instead of three. It commemorates the occasion when five kings – of Cyprus, Denmark, England, France and Scotland all dined together in 1363.

Winchester Palace stood in Southwark. It was almost completely destroyed in 1814, but you can still see a 14th-century rose window in what was the west gable of the great hall.

One o'clock clubs

One o'clock clubs are open on weekday afternoons and are for parents and their children under five. Parents must stay with their children, but they can relax and enjoy a cup of tea while the toddlers are kept happy and occupied by trained staff either out-of-doors in the playground or in the heated building. As the name suggests, one o'clock clubs are open from one until around four, and they are free.

For details of clubs run by the GLC, telephone 633 1633. Other clubs are organised by the local borough councils, and you can find out where there is one near you by contacting the information office at your local town hall, or the library, or get in touch with one o'clock club offices at 285 Albany Road SE5, [701 2046].

Orienteering

This is a cheap sport, and one that people of almost any age can take part in. You need to be able to run, although speed isn't the only thing that matters, and you need to be able to read a map. So, you're given a course, and the idea is to complete it by reaching various checkpoints, but the route is up to you.

Organisations

British Orienteering Federation, 41 Dale Road, Matlock, Derbyshire DE4 3LT, [Matlock 3661].

London Orienteering Club, Secretary, 44 Southview Road N8.

Orienteering courses

GLC parks with courses are at Bostall Heath and Woods, Castlewood, Hainault Forest and Oxleas Wood.

South-Eastern Orienteering Association has a permanent course on Hampstead Heath. Free maps are available for beginners living in Camden from the office at Parliament Hill or the Sports Development Officer, [278 4444, ext. 2134].

Event (*see* Calendar)

GLC Championships

Palaces

We all have romantic ideas of palaces and castles – all turret, moats and pinnacles, but London's palaces aren't like that at all. Most of them look like large houses, now sadly dwarfed by taller buildings that tower over them. Not only royalty lived in palaces. It's the name given to places where high dignitaries of the church live.

Places to visit

Buckingham Palace is the permanent home of the sovereign. You can tell if the Queen is in residence because if she is, the Royal Standard will be flying. It was actually built for the Duke of Buckingham 1702–5. Later it was bought for Queen Charlotte, and George IV inherited it. He decided to have vast alterations done to it, but died before it was completed, and so it was Queen Victoria who moved in.

Eltham Palace used to be very popular with the monarchy, but there's not much of it left now. You approach it by crossing a 14th-century bridge over a moat, and then you can stroll on the forecourt, and have a look at the restored Banqueting Hall with its oriel windows and magnificent hammerbeam roof.

Fulham Palace was the residence of the Bishop of London until 1973. The oldest part is the courtyard on the west side, and that's probably early 16th century. The rest was constructed in the 18th and 19th centuries.

Hampton Court Palace really does look like one. It was built in the early 16th century for Cardinal Wolsey, and he gave it to Henry VIII in an effort to regain his favour – not that it did any good. The king enlarged the building, and now you can see its courtyards, state apartments, the Chapel Royal, vast kitchens and grounds. (Refreshments; meals; picnic in grounds.)

 (King's Privy Garden, Great Fountain Gardens, Elizabethan Knot Gardens, Wilderness, Broad Walk only.)

Kensington Palace, when it was still only twenty-five years old, was bought by William III in 1689. He altered and enlarged it, and it became the home of the royal family for many years. It was here that Queen Victoria was born.

The state apartments, with many royal mementoes and some superb pictures, are open to the public, and so is the magnificent Orangery with its white-panelled walls, columns and classical statues. Don't leave without having a look at the charming sunken garden.

Lambeth Palace has been the home of Archbishops of Canterbury for over 750 years. It is entered through a Tudor red-brick gatehouse, built about 1490. Much of the palace was badly damaged in the Second World War, but it has been carefully restored. The Great Hall, 70 feet high, has a superb hammerbeam roof, very like the one in Westminster Hall. The palace is occasionally open to conducted parties by application to the Chaplain.

St James's Palace was built by Henry VIII, and other bits were added on as time went by, but in the early 1800s, part of it was burned down. It was built on the site of a leper hospital, and that is why foreign ambassadors are still accredited to the Court of St James. You can usually be admitted to the Ambassadors' Court and to services in the Chapel Royal from October to Palm Sunday.

Parks

London has more parks and open spaces than any other city, and each has its own special charm and character. If we haven't included your favourite park, it's because there just isn't enough room to put them all in.

Alexandra Park is a good park with lots for children to look at, and plenty of things to do with its pitch and putt course, lake, adventure playground and paddling pool, and a one o'clock club and workshop in the Grove.

Battersea Park was once a swamp, but when soil from the site of the Royal Victoria Docks was dumped there, it became a 200-acre park. It's a lively place with fairs, band concerts, dancing and exhibitions. It also has facilities for a wide variety of sports, and there's a playpark and a one o'clock club.
● See also p.35.

Blackheath was once a wild open common known as Bleack Heath, and a favourite haunt of 18th-century highwaymen. It has facilities for football, cricket, rounders and tennis, and it's a good place for flying kites.

Castlewood, Jackwood and Oxleas Wood cover almost 300 acres of woodland between Shooters Hill and Rochester Way in south-east London. The castle is the 18th-century Sevendroog Castle with steep terracing and a beautiful rose garden. You can wander peacefully through the woodland along a network of paths and tracks, or for the more energetic, there's a putting green, horse riding and pitches for football, cricket and netball.

Crystal Palace Park was named after the Crystal Palace which was moved from Hyde Park when the 1851 Great Exhibition closed, but it was destroyed by fire in 1936. One of its big attractions are the huge models of dinosaurs and other primaeval animals. There's lots to attract the young, including a one o'clock club and a playpark. The park is the home of the National Sports Centre. (Refreshments, March–October.)

Dulwich Park has lovely gardens with dazzling displays of rhododendrons and azaleas. You can putt, play cricket, football and netball, as well as take part in many other activities. (Rose garden; refreshments, lunches, February–October.)

Epping Forest stretches 10 miles from Epping to Chingford, and its 600 acres is a haven for wildlife. Boats can be hired on Connaught Water and Hollow Pond, and you can usually hire a pony at High Beach at weekends and during the school holidays. Sporting facilities include swimming at Whipps Cross Lido, football, cricket and golf.

Finsbury Park is one of London's oldest parks, and it has a typical Victorian layout. There's a lake, a putting green and bandstand, a one o'clock club, a playpark and a playground. Its sporting facilities include football, hockey, putting and tennis. (Refreshments, lunches, March–October.)

Green Park was once a rendezvous for duellists. Now it's a small informal park bright with crocuses and daffodils in the spring, but in the main it consists of unadorned greenery and trees. The Broad Walk, running from the Victoria Memorial in front of Buckingham Palace to Piccadilly, has ornamental gates at each end.

Greenwich Park, linked to the National Maritime Museum, houses the Old Royal Observatory. The eastern end of the park is a wild area of bracken and wild flowers. The north end is where all the action is. There's a boating lake, a children's playground, and a sandpit, as well as tennis courts.

Hainault Forest is all that's left of the Great Forest of Essex, but there's still about 1100 acres. If you don't know the forest very well, it's a good idea to stick to the signposted walks. For the very active, there's putting, two golf courses, a putting green, a riding track, cricket and football pitches, and you can fish in the lake.

(Foxburrows Farm Road, refreshments Easter–October.)
● See also p.35.

Hampstead Heath, Golders Hill Park, Parliament Hill and Kenwood cover over 800 acres. The heath alone offers miles of pleasant walks where foxes and other animals breed and where many species of birds can be spotted. There are lakes for fishing and swimming, and in Golders Hill Park there's a putting green and tennis courts. Parliament Hill has a pond where you can fish or sail boats, a playpark and a one o'clock club, and facilities for a wide variety of sports. It's a good kite-flying place too.
● See also pp.31, 175.

Holland Park was once the private grounds of Holland House, and it really is beautiful. The central section of the house was badly damaged in the Second World War, but it's been restored and converted into an open air theatre. It has a one o'clock club and a playpark, and you can play cricket and football, squash or tennis there.

(The Belvedere; licensed lunches, dinners.)

Hyde Park is London's best known park with 360 acres stretching from Park Lane to Kensington and Notting Hill Gate, and southwards from the Bayswater Road to Knightsbridge. Demonstrations, public meetings and marches are traditionally held here, and there's usually a crowd listening to soap-box orators at Speakers' Corner at Marble Arch. You can feed the ducks, fish, row or canoe on the Serpentine or skate if the ice is thick enough, and you can always ride in fashionable Rotten Row.

(Refreshments, lunches.)

Jubilee Gardens between County Hall and the Royal Festival Hall, was opened by the Queen in Jubilee Year. Although small, it's pleasant with its avenue of plane trees and sunken garden with a platform for concerts and dancing.

Kensington Gardens joins Hyde Park on the Kensington side, and is a favourite place for children, with the Round Pond and the playground with swings donated by J. M. Barrie, the creator of Peter Pan whose statue is there. The Elfin Oak is a tree stump brought from Richmond Park with lumps and bumps fashioned into animals, elves and pixies. There's the pets' cemetery to visit, lots of space to fly kites, and in August there are often puppet shows.

Lee Valley Park, which follows the course of the River Lee from Ware in Hertfordshire to London's east end, is the ideal place for the whole family with its multiplicity of sports and leisure activities. Large areas of water offer sailing, rowing, fishing and boat trips, and there are plenty of places to picnic on the river bank. You can follow a nature trail, go to the two sports centres, take part in riding, skating or swimming, or if you are interested in history, you can visit Rye House or Waltham Abbey. A Leisurebus operates on a circular route around the park, and on Sundays and Bank Holidays it links with the rail service from Liverpool Street Station.

Photography

Regent's Park is roughly circular in shape, and it's surrounded by beautiful houses designed by John Nash. It's the largest of the central London parks with the London Zoo in the north-west corner. Between the zoo and the outer circle is the main sports area with facilities for football, cricket, hockey, lacrosse, netball, archery and athletics, and instruction in golf. The inner circle contains Queen Mary's rose garden and the open air theatre. You can hire boats on the lake, and children can mess around in the separate pool.

Richmond Park consists of 2500 acres, and there's lots of wildlife to observe. If you feel active, you can ride, fish, or play football and cricket.

St James's Park is probably the prettiest of London's parks. The flower beds, shrubs and trees look lovely throughout the year. If you stand on the bridge of the lake, you'll have a marvellous view of Whitehall southwards and of Buckingham Palace to the north. The land was first acquired by Henry VIII and later Charles II had it laid out with avenues of trees and a canal. Subsequently, George IV had it replanted as an English country house garden. There's a playground with swings and a sandpit in one area of the park.

Even if you're not very good with a camera, you'll probably get pleasure out of looking at those taken by experts, and perhaps the more you look the more you'll learn about the art of photography.

Places to visit

Kingston Museum and Heritage Centre has a permanent display of the Eadweard Muybridge photographic collection.

Kodak Museum has the largest collection of photographic exhibits and equipment in the country. There are over 8,000 items on display. You can see optical toys, apparatus, magic lanterns and follow the history of photography. The picture gallery has a regularly changing photographic exhibition and an audio-visual presentation.

Photographer's Gallery, 8 Great Newport Street WC2, [836 7860] is open Tuesday–Saturday 11.00–18.00 and has frequently changing exhibitions.

Science Museum has early equipment on display, including relics of Fox Talbot and early Daguerrotype apparatus.
● See also p.157.

Playgroups

Playgroups are for children aged between three and five, although some take children who are slightly younger. Sessions last two or three hours in the morning or afternoon, and might be anything from two days a week to every day of the week. Usually they are only open during term time. Some playgroups are provided free of charge by a local borough, others are private and charge a fee – though there is usually help available for families who are really hard up.

Parents can leave their offspring in the care of the trained playgroup leaders, though they are encouraged to join in and help as much as possible. The aim is to widen the scope of young children and get them to mix with others. The children are kept busy with paints, books, bricks, puzzles, sand and water, climbing frames, and so on; and there's usually some organised story-telling, music making or dancing.

To find out where there's a playgroup in your area you can ask at your local library, clinic, or town hall information desk. Or you can get in touch with:

Organisations

British Association for Early Childhood Education, Montgomery Hall, Kennington, Oval SE11.

Pre-School Playgroup Association (PPA), Alford House, Aveline Street SE11, [582 8871].

Playparks

Playparks are areas within parks for anyone of school age, and are a bit like junior adventure playgrounds. Playleaders are around, helping to organise things and keeping a sharp eye on unorganised games. Most playparks have space where you can let off steam after school, with climbing structures, and a heated building for crafts and games such as table tennis.

Playparks are open after school, during the holidays and on Saturdays. There are often special activities with inflatables or open-air theatre. To find out if there is a playpark in your area ask at the town hall information office or at your local library.

For playparks organised by the GLC telephone 633 1633.

Pottery and porcelain

(*see also* Action holidays, Community centres)

A lot of people get a great deal of pleasure out of looking at pottery and porcelain, and quite a number would like to have a go at making pottery. Well, you can do both in London.

Taking part

Battersea Arts Centre has a pottery workshop for families on Sunday 11.00–12.30, 13.30–15.00. It's also included in its holiday programme.
● See also p.179.

Camden Arts Centre runs pottery classes at weekends and during the school holidays for those aged 7–16.
● See also p.179.

Chelsea Pottery has children's classes on Saturdays 10.00–13.00 and 14.00–17.00.

Geffrye Museum includes pottery in its Saturday workshop sessions.
● See also p.160.

Horham School has classes in all aspects of working clay, both for experienced potters and

beginners. Parents and children's classes are held on Wednesdays after school and on Saturday mornings.

Horniman Museum has pottery in its Saturday morning craft club.
● See also p.106.

Last Chance Centre has 2-hour pottery classes 3 times a week.

Museums

British Museum has marvellous examples of British, Medieval, Greek, Roman and Oriental ceramics.
● See also p.56.

Broomfield Museum has a permanent display of ceramics.
● See also p.140.

Fenton House has a marvellous collection of English and Continental porcelain, and in the Oriental Room there's really beautiful Chinese porcelain.
● See also p.139.

Martinware Pottery Collection includes birds, mugs, faces and other grotesque and amusing pieces.

Passmore Edwards Museum has a comprehensive collection of Bow porcelain.

● See also p.140.

Victoria and Albert Museum has an exhibition showing the development of ceramics through the ages. There's an impressive collection of Bow, Chelsea and Derby, and many examples of Oriental art. Modern ceramics can be bought in the craft shop.
● See also p.139.

Wallace Collection has an outstanding collection of European, Chinese and English porcelain.
● See also p.48.

Puppets

(*see also* Theatre)

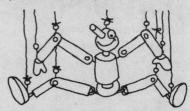

There has been a revival in the art of puppetry over the last few years, and now there are quite a lot of places where you can see shows or even learn how to make one.

Places to visit

Battersea Arts Centre is the home of the Puppet Centre. It has a small permanent exhibition and will help you to make puppets and put on a show.
● See also p.179.

Bethnal Green Museum of Childhood has a genuine Punch and Judy booth, made in 1912, an early 18th-century marionette theatre and a puppet collection.
● See also p.92.

Little Angel Marionette Theatre is London's permanent puppet theatre with shows at weekends and during the holidays. Performances last just over an hour and are for 3–6 year-olds at 11.00 on Saturday mornings. Afternoon shows are for older children. The theatre has been going for 20 years, and its puppets are among the finest ever made. It's also the venue for visiting companies both from this country and from abroad.

Nomad Puppets is a miniature theatre run by a family of puppeteers. There are two shows at weekends, and a puppet party show with games, prizes and tea. It's small and very friendly.

Polka Children's Theatre has a permanent exhibition of puppets of the world and runs puppet-making workshops, including magic, music and mime. It presents shows for children of all ages throughout the year, and lots of visiting companies appear there.

Puppet Theatre Barge is an old Thames barge converted into a floating theatre. From September to Easter it's moored at Camden Lock, and during the summer it moves to different places on the canal. There are shows for both under 5s and older children.

Unicorn Theatre includes puppet-making in its workshops.
• See also p.170.

GLC organises free puppet shows in the parks in the summer holidays. Watch noticeboards or telephone [633 1707] for information.

Event (see Calendar)

International Puppet Festival

Railways

(see also Travelling and sightseeing tours)

There are those who are devoted to the age of steam, and there are those who just love going on trains. Both groups are catered for in London.

Organisation

Rail Riders Club is British Rail's club for those aged 5–15. Once you've paid your membership fee, you'll receive a membership card, a badge, and a magazine crammed with information, competitions, and so on, and you'll be able to stick a detailed route-finder wallchart on your bedroom wall.

Places to visit

British Rail, whenever possible, takes parties behind the scenes to inspect engine sheds. There are also annual open days in depots like Stratford East and Selhurst where you can see locos and demonstrations showing how they are maintained. Find out about them by looking in your local press. For further information about visits and organised trips at Waterloo or Euston, write to the Public Affairs Manager. For Liverpool Street, write to HQ

York Y01 1HT, and for
Paddington to 125 House, 1
Gloucester Street, Swindon.

Royalty and Railways Exhibition
see Famous people (Madame
Tussaud's).

Science Museum has *Puffing Billy*,
the oldest locomotive in the world,
built in 1813, a cutaway replica of
Stephenson's *Rocket* so that you
can look at its inside, and the
Caerphilly Castle, a post-war loco.
Have a look at the working signal
box, early and up-to-date booking
offices, signalling equipment and
other railway equipment.
● See also p.157.

Southall Railway Centre has
seven restored locomotives, three
of them of GWR origin, two diesel
and two industrial engines in full
working order, and you can see
some of them in steam on Bank
Holiday and other weekends. The
GWR Preservation Group offers a
variety of interesting and inventive programmes, sometimes
combining visits to the centre with
trips to other places. The centre is
open for static display at weekends between Easter and the end
of November.

Thames Mini Cruises *see* Boats
(Boat trips).

Riding

At one time people were expected
to be properly kitted out if they
were going to ride – jodhpurs,
jacket and boots. Well, that's all
changed, but what you must have
is a hard hat – some stables lend
them – and you must wear
sensible boots or shoes.

Organisations

British Horse Society, British
Equestrian Centre, Stoneleigh,
Kenilworth, Warwickshire CV8,
[Coventry 52241] has information
about clubs, stables and events.

Pony Club of Great Britain, c/o
British Pony Club Office, British
Equestrian Centre (*see* above) is
for anyone who can read or ride.
Once you've become a member
you'll get newsletters, be able to
join one of its 369 pony clubs and
learn to look after ponies and take
part in games and other events.
You don't actually have to own a
pony to belong.

Places to ride

Places where you can ride include
Burgess Park, Dulwich Park,
Hackney Marsh, Hainault Forest,
Hampstead Heath Extension,
Hyde Park, Oxleas Wood,
Richmond Park, Streatham
Common and Trent Park.

Places to learn to ride

There are many good stables in London, including those listed below:

Bushey Park Riding School, Hampton Court Green, [979 1748]

Deen Farm Association *see* City farms

Fulham Community Sports programmes include riding. Telephone [748 3020] for further information.

Gillian's Riding School, Brayside Farm, Clay Hill, Enfield, Middlesex, [366 5445]

Holly Hill Riding Stables, The Ridgeway, Enfield, Middlesex, [366 5445]

Kentish Town City Farm *see* City farms

King's Oak Riding Stables, Theobalds Park Road, Enfield, Middlesex, [363 8620]

Kingston Riding Centre, 38A Crescent Road, Kingston, Surrey, [546 6361]

Lee Valley Park Centre, Lea Bridge Road, Leyton E10, [556 2629]

Michael Sobell Sports Centre for pony trecking.
● See also p.163.

Mudchute Community Farm *see* City farms

Roehampton Riding Stables, Roehampton Gate, Priory Lane SW15, [876 7089]

Events (*see* Calendar)

Royal Windsor Horse Show

Horse of the Year Show

Metropolitan Horse Show and Tournament

London Horse Harness Parade

Greater London Horse Show

Science and technology

The speed at which science advances is breathtaking, but it was also true during the Industrial Revolution. Whilst enjoying looking at the latest technological equipment, there's something to be said for having a look at the past and seeing how things developed.

Places to visit

Cuming Museum has some of the experimental scientific instruments belonging to Michael Faraday.
● See also p.40.

Faraday Laboratory and Museum is in the basement of the Royal Institute. The laboratory, now restored, looks as it did in 1845. The museum contains a unique collection of original apparatus.

Geological Museum presents The Story of the Earth, the largest programme on basic earth science in the world. You mustn't miss the erupting volcano. Using video film, it simulates the real thing, rumbling ominously. Best of all is the earthquake, with the floor jolting and juddering, just as if you're in the middle of the real thing. (*see* Natural History, Science and Victoria and Albert Museums.)

IBA Broadcasting Gallery illustrates the development of television and radio in a series of interesting displays, including sound recordings, and it gives you a good idea of how television works and what goes to make up a programme. There's also a lively account of how *News at Ten* appears on the screen. Do note that these conducted tours are only for those over the age of 16, and that they must be made by prior appointment.

Light Fantastic Gallery of Holography presents an amazing display of 3D light laser pictures.

London Planetarium has one hour laserium shows of multi-coloured pulsating images produced by a krypton gas laser and 2000 watts of sound, all combining in a brilliant but incredibly noisy laser light concert.
● See also p.49.

Molecule Theatre is quite different from any other theatrical show. Operating at the Mermaid Theatre, it puts on programmes of ingenious scientific entertainment for those aged 7–12, but there are occasional performances for younger children. These really are fun shows.

National Maritime Museum has a large collection of early scientific instruments.
● See also p.55.

Science Museum has so many exhibits that it's impossible to list them. It has everything ranging from a mock-up coal mine to a lunar module. The gadgets in the Children's Gallery will keep compulsive knob twiddlers and button addicts busy for ages. Have a go at the device for producing electricity. Turn a handle as rapidly as possible, and after 15 seconds, a VDU will show you how much current you've generated and what it would cost.

There are impressive displays on telecommunications technology ranging from an 1850 telegraph office to today's Prestel and radio paging, and the development of calculating devices and computers. There's even a computer terminal for you to operate. (Refreshments.)

Telecom Technology Showcase has unique displays, videos and working models, bringing over 200 years of telecommunications history to life, and giving you a good idea of what the future might hold. See early telegraphs, switchboards and telephones, and examine today's equipment. There's Prestel, satellite communication, and lots of other exhibits, some of which you can operate. Do note that this is only for those over the age of 7.

Thames Barrier at Silvertown in Woolwich Reach is designed to exclude surge tides from the upper estuary, thus preventing London from flooding. It's constructed of a series of movable gates built side by side. When not in use, they rest out of sight in curved concrete housings in the river bed, so there's free passage for river traffic.

Trocadero has a new Light Fantastic Hologram exhibition.

Signs

There are, of course, so many street signs that it's impossible to list them, but as you wander around London, you might spot these.

Places to visit

City of London lampposts have different signs. Some have a shield and a dagger, part of the arms of the City; others have signs indicating the parish that you are in.

Cuming Museum has the 'Dog and Pot' shop sign.
● See also p.40.

Guildhall Museum has pilgrim signs and badges, and shop and tavern signs.
● See also p.120.

Lombard Street has a lot of street signs.

The Mall has small 14th-century ships with square sails on its lampposts.

Old Bailey has Justice on the top. She's holding a sword and scales in her hands.
● See also p.131.

14 Princes Gate has Indian heads over the windows. It used to be the official residence of the United States Ambassador.

Royal Exchange has a golden grasshopper 11 feet long. The grasshopper was the family crest of Sir Thomas Gresham, its founder.
● See also p.123.

St Clement Dane's has a weather vane with an anchor incorporated in the design. That's because St Clement is the patron saint of sailors. In fact, the vicarage is actually called the Anchorage.

St Lawrence Jewry has a gridiron on the top of its spire. That's because that's how St Lawrence met his death.

St Mary-le-Bow has a griffin for a weather vane on top of its campanile.

St Nicholas Cole Abbey has a sailing ship for a weather vane.

Trafalgar Square has the Standard Yard, a length of bronze, built into the north wall of the fountains' enclosure.
● See also p.122.

Skiing

You don't have to go abroad these days to find out if you'll be any good at skiing. You can have a go at one of London's artificial ski slopes.

Organisation

National Ski Federation of Great Britain, 118 Eaton Square SW1, [235 8227] has a list of all British dry ski slopes.

Places to ski

Alexandra Palace Ski Slope, at the aerial end of the park, is open Monday–Friday 19.00–22.00, and at weekends and during the school holidays 14.00–22.00.

Blue Sky Ski Centre is open Monday–Friday and Sundays 10.00–22.00, Saturdays 10.00–17.00. Ring for details of Saturday morning beginners' courses.

Crystal Palace Ski Centre is open Monday–Saturday 13.30–21.00, Sunday 9.30–16.00. It runs pre-ski, and beginners' courses, and has children's practice mid-week. If you are under 13, you must be accompanied by an adult.

Michael Sobell Sports Centre has courses for beginners on its Mogul Slope ski-training machine.
● See also p.163.

Woolwich Ski Slope is open Monday–Friday 10.00–22.00, and at weekends 10.00–17.00. There are also children's courses and practice sessions. Ring for details.

Social history

(*see also* Costumes)

London's an exciting place to live in the 1980s, but what was it like in times gone by? There are several places you can visit to see what everyday life was like at different periods in history.

Museums

Chiswick House, an early 18th-century villa, and a grand one at that, is superbly decorated and furnished in the style of the time. (Café in grounds.)

Church Farm House Museum, chiefly concerned with the history of Hendon, has rooms decorated and furnished in period style.

Geffrye Museum has a fascinating series of period rooms displaying furniture, panelling and domestic equipment which illustrates the development of middle-class English homes from about 1600. There's also a reconstructed 18th-century woodworker's shop and an open hearth kitchen.

(Refreshments, picnic in gardens.)

Grange Museum gives you a glimpse of the lives of the ordinary people of Wembley and Willesden. It has a 1930s lounge, a Victorian parlour, and an Edwardian draper's shop. (Picnic in garden.)

Gunnersbury Park Museum is the place to see what Victorian kitchens were like. Imagine working in one. The museum often has permanent and temporary exhibitions related to social work.
● See also p.76.

Linley Sambourne House is quite unique. It reflects the taste of those living in the late Victorian and Edwardian eras.

● See also p.46.

Museum of London will give you a really vivid idea of how Londoners have lived ever since the city was founded. Every period is covered, right up to what it was like during the blitz.
● See also p.40.

National Museum of Labour History has a permanent exhibition showing the history of the Labour Party. There's a display of trade union banners which illustrates the pride working men and women took in their skills.

Osterley Park House is a mansion, built in 1711 and redesigned by Robert Adam. All the decorations and furnishings were either designed or chosen by him, and it will give you a good idea of how the rich of the late 18th century lived.

Science Museum illustrates the way that science and technology have eased the work of housewives with displays of cooking, heating, cleaning and washing apparatus from many periods. There's a replica of an 1880s kitchen and bathroom – not much like those of today.
● See also p.157.

Sports and leisure centres

The number of sports centres in London continues to increase, and because so many different sporting activities go on all under one roof, you're bound to find something that appeals to you. Sports centres are usually open all day and every day, with special clubs and activities for different age groups, and very often additional programmes during school holidays. Ring the individual centre for precise information about opening times and activities.

Abbey Wood Sports Centre has a swimming pool with sub-aqua facilities, a sports hall and courts for ball games. There are special activities for under-12s on Saturday afternoons and during school holidays, and for over-12s in the evenings after school.

Britannia Leisure Centre has weekend and after-school activities for children from the age of four, and for toddlers there's a range of soft equipment and adventure toys, where the future champions can flex their muscles! The school holiday programmes include gymnastics, trampolining, squash, badminton, table-tennis, five-a-side, judo and basketball. Occasionally there's an ice-skating day on synthetic ice tiles.

Bullsmoor Sports Centre offers gymnastics, trampolining, martial arts and keep fit in the gymnasium; badminton and squash on the courts. Outside there's a floodlit all-weather playing area, tennis courts and a netball court. You can even have your birthday party there, with games, races, trampolining and so on to amuse your friends.

Crystal Palace National Sports Centre has a wide range of activities for children, including summer holiday courses. There are courts for badminton and squash, an indoor cricket school, outdoor facilities for field events, an all weather playing area, and an international standard swimming pool. The centre is also the home of the Southeast England division of the Sports Council.

Eastway Sports Centre has Baby Bounce for toddlers, and for juniors, gymnastics, short tennis,

table tennis, badminton, etc. There's also a unique, enclosed cycle circuit.
● See also p.62.

Elephant and Castle Recreation Centre consists of a sports complex and a leisure pool. There are facilities for most sports.
● See also p.166.

Ferndale Sports Centre has all the usual sports facilities, and during the school holidays has a very good playscheme for children aged 5–15. As well as sports activities, there are arts and crafts and organised trips.

Flaxman Sports Centre has weekly sessions for children in ballet, tap, modern dance and movement, gymnastics and trampoline. Holiday activities are for 5–15 year-olds.

George Green Sports Centre has facilities for most sports and classes in trampoline, table tennis, judo, martial arts, archery.

George Sylvester Sports Centre has activities after school and at weekends, including judo, roller skating, five-a-side, trampolining, badminton, short tennis and table tennis.

Hillingdon Youth Sports Centre has sessions for 7–11 year-olds,

and a wide-ranging programme for 11–16s. Activities and training on offer include archery, badminton, basketball, cricket, circuit training and so on. What's more, if a sport's not available at the centre, they will help you find a place that does do it.
● See also p.51.

Jubilee Hall Recreation Centre has two unusual activities on offer – acrobatics and juggling! There's also the more conventional sports such as roller-skating, badminton, volleyball, table tennis, martial arts and so on.
● See also p.51.

Kelmscott Leisure Centre runs the Kelmscotter Kids Club for 5–12 year-olds on Saturday mornings. 12–16 year-olds can participate in a wide range of sports after school.

Leytonstone Recreation Centre has a multigym, squash courts, and all-weather floodlit training area. For swimmer's there's a learner pool and a main pool.

London Central YMCA has a junior programme for 8–16 year-olds after school and at weekends. There's family swimming at weekends, but children must bring an adult member with them.
● See also p.179.

Michael Sobell Sports Centre runs a Saturday club where 6–16 year-olds can take part in a wide range of activities, and there are special holiday programmes. Under-5s can enjoy Baby Bounce on weekday afternoons. There's also an ice rink, a Mogulslope ski trainer, and a snooker room.

Mornington Sports Centre has a junior club on Sundays, and during the week classes in gymnastics, football and trampolining.

Picketts Lock Centre has Baby Bounce and a Ducklings swimming class for under-5s, and for the rest of the family there's swimming, roller-skating, trampoline, table tennis, tennis, netball, squash, badminton, golf, football, and there's instruction available in most sports. There is a small membership fee, and then you pay individually for whatever activity you're taking part in.
● See also p.62.

Plumstead Sports Centre has boys' and girls' clubs for gymnastics, and leagues in soccer, netball and hockey. There are all sorts of activities during the holidays, and gentle gymnastics for the under-5s during termtime.

Swiss Cottage Sports Centre has a sports hall for most sports, an outdoor area and two swimming pools. There are lessons in swimming, diving, sub-aqua, synchronised swimming, acrobatics – and a fun session with a gigantic suspended spider.

Tottenham Sports Centre has a Kids Club on Saturday mornings where you can do all kinds of sport. There's also football coaching and roller-skating during the week after school.

Vale Farm Sports Centre is set in beautiful parkland and there are extensive playing fields as well as an athletic track. There's also a sports hall, squash courts, a polygym with a cycle machine, a 25-metre swimming pool and a learner pool, and giant chess. There are clubs after school and at weekends, and a holiday programme with many coaching courses in a wide range of sports.

Walnuts Sports Centre in Orpington has facilities for most sports and a swimming pool.

Wanstead Leisure Centre has courses in judo, badminton, trampoline, karate and football after school and on Saturdays, and during school holidays. On Sunday afternoons there's a dance club and roller-skating, and the centre will soon have a 200-seat theatre for plays.

Wapping Sports Centre has facilities for most sports, and a holiday programme.

Stamps

(*see also* Guided tours)

Most people collect something, but a surprising number of people collect stamps. For them, there's a great deal that they can do in London.

There are, of course, shops selling stamps. One of the best places to browse around is The Arches, open during normal shopping hours. It's actually a pedestrian underpass beneath Charing Cross, and there are a number of stalls and small shops, specialising in stamps, coins and medals.

Organisations

National Philatelic Society, 1 Whitehall Place SW1, [839 1987] is open to those over the age of 16, but it will accept slightly younger people if they are really keen. There's a quarterly magazine and meetings with talks, competitions and exhibitions. There's a library, the committee answers members' queries, and once a year it organises a competition for children.

Stamp Bug Club, Freepost, PO Box 94, Darly House, Redhill, Surrey runs an interesting scheme sponsored by the post office. For a small membership fee, you'll get *Stamp Bug News*, a colourful eight-page newspaper eight times a year, and this will help you to keep up-to-date with British stamps.

Museums

Bruce Castle Museum tells the history of the development of the postal services. This is an apt place to mount such an exhibition since Sir Rowland Hill, the father of the post office, lived here 1827–33. The many exhibits include a collection of Victorian pillar boxes and postmarks. (Picnic in grounds.)

National Postal Museum probably has the most important and extensive collection of stamps in the world. It has proof sheets of virtually every British stamp issued since 1840, the Phillips collection, and the Berne collection of stamps from member countries of the Universal Postal Union. The museum also mounts two special exhibitions a year.

Event (*see* Calendar)

Stampex

Swimming

There are plenty of places to swim all over London. Local borough indoor pools can be found in the telephone directory, listed under public baths, so they are not included. Most have swimming clubs and classes, and often duckling sessions for under-5s and their parents. If you're a regular swimmer, ask if there's a season ticket since this will save you money. Some sports centres have a pool open to non-members, but it will cost you more to enter than subscribers.

Leisure pools are a new idea, and are beginning to take over from conventional pools. They are often irregular in shape, with a gentle shelving bottom like a beach. There are wave machines, palm trees, slides – all at a temperature much higher than ordinary pools, and they provide a complete day out for all the family.

The idea that pools need not be just for swimming is catching on in some council baths. Waterfun is meant for people who can already swim, and you can mess around with inflatables, rubber tyres, and so on – a sort of adventure playground in the water.

Water fun is available at the following places:

Islington: Merlin Street Baths, [837 1313]; Caledonian Road Baths, [837 0852] (during school holidays)

Lambeth: Clapham Pool, [622 2786]; Streatham Pool, [769 6971] (during school holidays)

Tower Hamlets: Poplar Baths, [987 3235] (Saturdays)

Waltham Forest: Leyton Baths, [539 2048]; Leytonstone Recreation Centre, [539 8343]

Organisations

Amateur Swimming Association, Harold Fern House, Derby Square, Loughborough, Leicestershire, [0509 230431]

British Sub-Aqua Club, 16 Upper Woburn Place WC1, [387 9302]

Leisure pools

Britannia Leisure Centre has a leisure pool with a wave-making machine and a tiled beach.
● See also p.161.

Broxbourne Lido is in Lee Valley Park and is one of the most modern in south-east England with artificial waves, underwater lighting, a fountain, a spray curtain and a simulated beach – all surrounded by exotic tropical plants and vines. There's plenty of room for sunbathing on the riverside terrace, and there's a UVA solarium.

Elephant and Castle Recreation Centre has a leisure pool with a large shallow water area and a wave-making machine. There's a children's splash pool with a pink elephant slide in a tropical

atmosphere, and a teaching pool.

Fulham Pools take the youngest member of the family very much into account. There are playpens by the poolside, nappy-changing benches and high chairs in the restaurant.

White City Pool has a pool with sloping sides and a wave machine with all sorts of facilities installed with the whole family in mind.

Outdoor swimming

If you're one of those tough types, you can swim in the Hampstead ponds all the year round. For the rest of us, the following lidos are open in the summer months:

Brockwell Lido, Brockwell Park SE24, [274 7991].

Eltham Park South Baths SE9, [850 9898].
● See also p.31.

Kennington Lido, Kennington Park SE11, [735 3574].

Parliament Hill Lido NW5, [485 3873].

Ruislip Lido, Reservoir Road, Ruislip, [Ruislip 34081].
● See also pp.000.

Serpentine Lido, Hyde Park W2.
● See also pp.000.

Southbury Road Recreation Centre, Enfield, Middlesex, [363 3065].

Victoria Park Lido E9, [985 6774].

Whipps Cross Lido, Whipps Cross Road E11, [989 1046].

Tennis

Many London parks have hard courts open throughout the year. In general, grass courts are used only in the spring and summer. If you intend to play frequently on a GLC court, then you should become a registered player. This is quite cheap, and it does mean that you can book a court in advance instead of hanging around and hoping that one might become free.

Organisations

Lawn Tennis Association, Palliser Road W14, [385 2366] has information about clubs and coaching schemes.

Middlesex Lawn Tennis Association, Secretary, 85 Watford Way NW4 will have information about local clubs.

Coaching and competitions

GLC runs coaching schemes in some London parks. Watch noticeboards for information or write to GLC Parks Department for a copy of *Tennis Coaching and Competitions*.

Hammersmith and Fulham run a series of 6-week junior courses in the summer holidays and an Easter holiday course. There are junior tournaments, weekend junior tournaments, and short tennis with equipment provided for over-5s. Local libraries will have information.

Hillingdon Sports Centre has expert coaching on a fast playing surface for those aged 14 and upwards.

Hounslow has tennis coaching in the summer holidays for those over the age of 12 provided they bring their own raquets and wear tennis shoes. Telephone [570 7728, ext. 3145] for information, or ask in local libraries.

Islington runs tennis coaching sessions at the beginning of the summer holidays. Ring the Recreation Department, [607 7331] for details, or ask at libraries.

Lambeth Amenity Services has set up a local tennis singles league to give players a chance to compete and improve their play. Telephone [622 6655, ext. 323] for further information.

London Parks and Clubs Lawn Tennis Association has a junior singles event for those under the age of 18 in its Greater London Tournaments. You must play tennis regularly within a 25-mile radius of Charing Cross to take part.

Richmond upon Thames runs a 3-day youth tennis tournament during the summer holidays for those aged under 14 and for 14–18 year-olds. You'll find entry forms in local libraries.

Tower Hamlets organises tennis coaching sessions during the summer holidays at the George Green Sports Centre. Telephone [247 1286] for information about its Action Sports Tennis Club at the Spitalfields (Brady) Centre.

Waltham Forest has coaching sessions at various parks during the summer holidays. Telephone [521 7111] for further information. It's also worth knowing that from October to March the courts are free.

London Transport excursion

London Transport organises an excursion trip to Wimbledon. The coach takes you to the tennis championships, you get a ticket so that you don't have to queue. You are given a packed lunch complete with strawberries, cream and wine, and there's also a free entrance ticket to the tennis museum. Included is a voucher for the bus to Southfields and an underground ticket back to central London. It's not cheap, but it's the easiest way of seeing Wimbledon. Note that there's a reduction for children and OAPs. Seats can be booked at London Transport Travel Enquiry Offices at Wilton Road Coach Station or from the Tours and Charter Manager, 55 Broadway SW1H 0BD.

Museum

Wimbledon Tennis Museum gives an absorbing picture of the origins and development of lawn tennis. You'll see clothes and equipment, a Victorian Parlour, the original Gentlemen's Dressing Room, lots of photographs, and film shows of great matches.

Event (*see* Calendar)

Wimbledon Fortnight

Theatre

Whether you aim to be the star of the show, or whether you just enjoy watching others perform, London is full of opportunities for those interested in the theatre. As well as all the places listed below, many community centres have drama workshops – and if acting isn't your scene, you might well be interested in lighting, costumes or stage management.

Taking part

Anna Scher Children's Theatre is one of the most exciting and active groups in London, but there's a long waiting list. Members are split into age groups from 6 to 21. Membership is cheap, but if your family is really hard up, you'll be unlikely to be turned away. It puts on 2 productions a year, and it also acts as an agency – some of the kids have taken part in *Grange Hill*.

Battersea Arts Centre does drama, mime and improvisation on Saturday mornings, and organises special activities in the school holidays. There are very moderate charges, and you pay for each session individually.
● See also p.179.

Curtain Theatre organises workshops for London schools, and it also runs The Curtain Raisers, a group of 14–18 year-olds, who meet on Wednesday and Friday evenings during term time.

De Leon Drama School runs a summer course for those aged 10–15.

Greenwich Young People's Theatre has drama workshops for 7–11 year-olds and those aged 11–13 after school on weekdays, and youth theatre projects for those over 14, working on productions for public performances. It has a visual arts workshop for older people, where you can learn about stage and costume design.

Group 64 Youth Theatre is a well run group strictly for those over 15 who want to develop their talents as an actor or use supporting skills such as design and lighting. There's no audition or test, and you'll be sure of a warm welcome. It has a 160-seat theatre, a rehearsal studio and a green room.

Half Moon Young People's Theatre has drama workshops for those aged 8–13 and 14–20.

Heatham House has one of London's most successful youth groups, putting on shows several times a year, and occasionally touring abroad with them.

Lauderdale House has workshops after school for those aged 5–12 and 12–15.

Mountview Youth Theatre has a Saturday morning drama workshop and a Saturday afternoon dance workshop for those aged 6–8 and 9–12. There are drama courses for teenagers in the evenings.

National Youth Theatre auditions those aged 14–20. You have to give 2 speeches of your own choice, one from Shakespeare and the other from a modern play. There are courses for juniors aged 14–17 and seniors aged 17–20, as well as production and technical tuition.

Polka Children's Theatre holds workshops in drama, mime, magic, stage make-up, toy theatres and costume. They're either on a one-off basis, or you can go on a course for a whole term. There are also holiday clubs and courses.
● See also p.153.

Questors Theatre has drama for 5–9, 10–14 and 15–17 year-olds on Saturday mornings and every weekday evening. The classes are mainly in improvisation, but shows are put on in the main theatre. There's a moderate charge on a weekly basis. If you're interested, put your name down as soon as possible – there's a long waiting list.

Royal Court Young People's Theatre organises practical activities for those aged 16–23, and is concerned with the writer/actor relationship. There's a waiting list, and when a vacancy occurs, the applicant goes along to a workshop to see what it's like.

They are keen to have people from all kinds of backgrounds.

St George's Theatre has workshops and holiday schemes. For secondary school pupils, there are all-day workshops on Shakespeare's plays.

Shaw Theatre has occasional workshops for children.

Stepney Youth Theatre has a drama workshop for those over 14, which meets every Thursday evening.

Tricycle Theatre has a drama workshop.
● See also p.172.

Unicorn Theatre has a theatre club during weekends and school holidays with various workshops – magic, make-up, masks, tumbling, scene-painting, make-a-play, and so on. It also puts on special productions for children.

Upstream Children's Theatre has children's workshops involving theatre games, clowning and other activities on Tuesdays 16.00–17.30 and Saturdays 13.00–15.00. Parents should ring if their children want to join, and preferably accompany them for the first visit.
● See also p.172.

Watching

Barbican Centre organises children's shows on public holidays, and there's an annual family festival each summer.
● See also p.101.

Battersea Arts Centre has a weekly children's show on Sundays at 15.30.
● See also p.179.

Bubble Theatre is a mobile group touring parks in Greater London through the summer, putting on a variety of plays for different age groups in a gaily-coloured bubble tent. Ring for details of places and times.

Common Stock Theatre is a community group putting on summer shows all over London and offering live entertainment to people who wouldn't normally go to the theatre.

Croydon Warehouse Theatre has regular Saturday morning shows at 11.00, often using puppets. Temporary membership is amazingly cheap.

Half Moon Young People's Theatre puts on shows at various venues around London during the summer.
● See also p.169.

Inter-Action Trust's Professor Dogge's Troupe works in parks, playgrounds, schools and community centres. Dolls' shows, using child-sized dolls, are popular with under-5s, and Animobile – a farmyard on wheels – brings city children into contact with animals. For older children, the Radio Van provides the opportunity to make, report and broadcast news programmes, using recording and printing equipment.
● See also p.78.

Intimate Theatre has Saturday morning shows at 11.15, with the audience encouraged to participate. The cost of a seat includes a raffle ticket.

Lauderdale House has Saturday morning children's shows at 11.30.
● See also p.169.

Lyric Theatre stages shows of all kinds – clowns, puppets and plays on Saturday mornings at 11.00.

Molecule Theatre *see* Science technology.

National Theatre has special shows for the young, especially at Christmas.
● See also p.172.

Polka Children's Theatre is particularly good for young children, since it specialises in mime, puppets, music and magic.
● See also p.153.

Riverside Studios put on shows for 2–12 year-olds on either Saturdays or Sundays at 12.30, while parents can relax in the bar or restaurant.

St George's Theatre has Saturday performances for those aged 6–11 at 14.30.
● See also p.170.

Shaw Theatre has a Saturday morning children's theatre club 10.30–12.30. The programme includes a show, a special guest, and a cliffhanger serial.

Tramshed Theatre usually has a children's show just before Christmas. Children are welcome at the Friday–Sunday cabarets, but must pay the adult price.

Tricycle Theatre has Saturday afternoon shows for those aged 4–12.

Unicorn Theatre has plays for 4–12 year-olds at weekends and during the school holidays, and its touring group performs in parks and playgrounds in the summer.
● See also p.170.

Upstream Children's Theatre performs for 5–12 year-olds in the school holidays. For those taking CSE and O-levels, there are plays followed by sessions when the cast talk about the characters and how the plays are presented.

Young Vic has a regular season of plays, musicals and other events suitable for young people. Saturday matinées begin at 14.30.

Open air theatre

Regent's Park Theatre is the place to see Shakespeare and other classical plays from June to August.

Backstage

Barbican Centre has fascinating backstage tours given by the Royal Shakespeare Company. These last 45–60 minutes. Telephone for times of tours and for booking.
● See also p.101.

National Theatre offers interesting tours backstage and through the workshop areas. These last about 75 minutes. Ring for times of tours and for booking.

Places to visit

Bear Gardens Museum of the Shakespearean Stage has models and contemporary material illustrating 16th- and 17th-century Bankside where Londoners watched performances at the Globe, Rose, Hope or Swan. There are models and plans for the reconstruction of the Globe, lecture tours, workshops and drama programmes. The Theatre, a full-size replica of an early 17th-century playhouse, is used for amateur and professional performances.

Museum of London's theatrical exhibits include life-size figures of Grimaldi, Kean and Irving, as well as music hall characters, all wearing authentic costumes.
● See also p.40.

St Paul's Church in Covent Garden is known as the actors' church. Some famous people have been buried there, and on the walls are memorials to many more.

Theatre Museum, opening in 1986 in Covent Garden, will house part of the Victoria and Albert Museum's theatrical collection.

Events (see Calendar)

Cutting of the Baddeley Cake
Grimaldi Commemoration Service

Travelling and sightseeing tours

There are quite a lot of cheap ways of getting in and out of London, and of seeing the capital. Some of the services mentioned below might have a curtailed winter service or vary times of tours. Check at the London Tourist Board, London Transport Enquiry Centres (*see* Information and information centres) or get in touch with individual tour operators.

British Rail

BR has so many bargains that it's almost confusing.

Family Railcards (currently £12) allow the railcard holder and two other adults to buy 2nd class single and return or Awayday return tickets at half the normal adult fare; up to four children can travel at the same time for a flat fare of £1 each, but even if they would normally all travel free, at least one must pay £1.

Triple Tickets offer three separate day trips from London that may be taken at any time within a month, taking in places like Winchester, Oxford, Cambridge, Hastings, Bristol,

King's Lynn and Salisbury. It's extraordinarily cheap (currently £15) with children paying half fare. Tickets are available from BR Travel Centres in London, London Tourist Board Offices, and at Gatwick and Heathrow airports.

London Transport tickets and tours

Tickets for all London Transport Tours can be bought at London Transport Enquiry Offices, but in some cases you pay as you board the bus or coach.

Golden Rovers can be bought on Green Line coaches or London and County buses Monday–Friday after 9.00. They give you the opportunity of using its 2000 mile network within one day (not route 747).

London Explorer is one of the best ways of seeing London. It gives unlimited travel on all red buses and tubes (not beyond Northwood, Queen's Park or Woodford on the Epping line), and you can buy 1-, 3-, 4-, or 7-day tickets. You'll be given a free mini-guide of London's main

attractions with details of how to reach them, and money-off vouchers for other London Transport tours, souvenirs and entry to the London Transport Museum.

London Transport Day Tours offer a comfortable seat in a modern coach with a friendly and experienced guide. Although not cheap, the price includes all admission charges and lunch. The tour includes the Changing of the Guard and guided tours round St Paul's Cathedral, Westminster Abbey and the Tower of London. The trip usually starts from Wilton Road Coach Station (not far from Victoria Station) on Tuesday, Wednesday, Friday and Saturday at 10.00.

London Transport Guided Coach Tours begin at Wilton Road Coach Station daily at 10.00 and 14.00. The morning tour takes in Westminster Abbey and the West End and is timed so that you'll see either the Changing of the Guard at Buckingham Palace or Horse Guards. The afternoon tour concentrates on the City and includes a guided tour of St Paul's Cathedral and the Tower of London.

London Transport 2-Hour Guided Tour is a daily (summer) non-stop double-decker bus trip starting from either Victoria (Grosvenor Gardens) or Piccadilly Circus at 9.30, 11.30 and 14.30. As you rumble past the most famous landmarks, a guide will identify them and tell you of their history. There's no need to book, just pay as you get on.

Red Rovers are a marvellous bargain. London Transport's buses roll along more than 1700 miles of road, and you can use them as much as you want for a whole day. Up to two children under the age of 5 go along free with each fare-paying passenger.

Round London Sightseeing Tours last 2 hours and cover about 20 miles, giving you the chance to see practically every building of importance. Although there's no guide, a free map will help you to identify places. All you have to do is to hop on at Victoria (Grosvenor Gardens), Piccadilly Circus or Marble Arch. The service operates once an hour, 7 days a week, 10.00–16.00.

Other tours

Culture Bus covers about 18 miles trundling through central London and the City. You can hop off at any stop, nip into a shop or explore a building, and jump on the next one that's passing, without paying any extra fare. The bus runs daily 9.00–18.00, but if you happen to have bought a ticket after 17.00, you can use it the next day. There are 20 stops in all, allowing you to see most of the major sights and the most important museums.

London Cityrama Sightseeing Tour has a taped commentary in 8 languages (English too), and they're synchronised as you pass the most important tourist attractions. The tour runs hourly from Grosvenor Gardens, the National Gallery, Piccadilly Circus and Westminster Abbey.

Telephone for details of timetable. This trip is free for children under the age of 3.

London Crusader Sightseeing shows you London with the help of a qualified guide. There are two tours, both using double-decker coaches, and you'll have a 2-hour trip around the most interesting parts of London and the City. If you don't mind making your way home, you can have a combined tour/Madame Tussaud's ticket, in which case you'll be dropped at the famous waxworks. Coaches pick passengers up at Marble Arch (Cumberland Hotel), Harrington Gardens (Gloucester Hotel), and Victoria. There's also an unguided tour. If you take this one, you're given a free map to help you to identify places.

Richmond Heritage Rides are on open-top buses which run an hourly service connecting Kew Gardens with Hampton Court Palace, passing all major tourist attractions and allowing you to get on and off as often as you like. Telephone [844 0944] for information.

Viewpoints

If you are feeling superior or on top of the world, why not go to one of these viewpoints and gaze over London's rooftops, or stare down at people scuttling around like ants. On the other hand, you might be feeling tranquil, in which case you can find a view that will echo your mood.

Places to visit

Alexandra Palace, built in 1873, but partially destroyed by fire later, dominates Muswell Hill. From its 250-foot high terraces, you'll get a fine view over north London, Essex and Hertfordshire.

Archway Bridge in Hornsey Lane, Highgate straddles the Archway Road. Traffic down below looks a bit like dinky toys.

Bostall Heath and Lesnes Abbey Woods gives a new dimension to the Thames. Just north of Lesnes Abbey, Plumstead marshes stretch away to the Thames, and if you've got sharp eyes, you'll see small ships looking as if some mysterious hand is dragging them along.

Hampstead Heath, at its highest point, is 450 feet above sea level. If you stand on the opposite side of the road from Whitestone Pond, you'll get an impressive view of London.
● See also p.147.

Heathrow Airport offers keen plane spotters the chance to see aircraft constantly taking off and landing. Go to the Spectators' Roof Garden above the Queen's building. You'll find it's got a small playground and a café. Remember, though, that in an emergency, it might be closed.

Island Gardens, on the Isle of Dogs, offers a stunning view across the river to the Royal Naval College.

Monument, the memorial built by Sir Christopher Wren to commemorate the Great Fire of 1666, is 202 feet high, the exact distance from the base of the Monument to the shop in Pudding Lane where it all started. If you're inclined to become dizzy, don't go up the spiral stairs. There are 311 of them.

● See also p.97.

St Paul's Cathedral offers a bird's eye view of the City. The height from the pavement to the top of the cross is 365 feet, and if you actually make it to the Ball and Cross, you'll have climbed 627 steps. Once there, you can walk around both inside and outside the dome. The dome is actually the famous Whispering Gallery. It's 420 feet in circumference, and if you stand close to the wall on one side and whisper, someone on the far side will be able to hear you.

● See also p.123.

Tower Bridge's lattice walkway provides a unique view of the Thames.

● See also p.61.

Westminster Cathedral, not far from Victoria station, has a 284-foot-high tower. You can either plod up the stairs or use a bit of pocket money to whizz up in the lift (this includes entry to the Sacristy as well). When you come down, spare a few minutes to look around. The cathedral is Byzantine in style, quite unlike anything else in London.

Walks

Londoners are luckier than many other city dwellers. There are parks and open spaces to stroll in, and pleasant stretches of the Thames to amble along, as well as other places to visit.

Walking on your own

Canal Walks are a pleasant way of passing the time. If you go west from Kensal Green, there's free access to the towpath at all times, but if you go east, you must remember that the gates are locked at night. Roughly speaking, they are open from about 9.00 to dusk. However, parts are very isolated, and you'd be foolish to go on your own. Take an adult or go in a group, and make sure that you stick together. Whatever you do, don't be stupid. Scuffling around on the towpath, even if it's meant to be fun, can be very dangerous. Use your head as well as your feet.

There are six possible walks: Salmon Lane Lock–Camden Town (nearly 6 miles); Camden Town–Little Venice (2½ miles); Little Venice–Willesden Junction (over 3 miles); Willesden Junction–Bull's Bridge, Southall (9½ miles); Brentford Lock–Hayes (5 miles); Hayes–Uxbridge (over 5 miles).

London Wall Walk *see* Archaeology.

Richmond upon Thames has produced *Exploring Richmond upon Thames* suggesting a series of walks in the area.

Silver Jubilee Walkway is a 5½-mile long pedestrian trail taking you across London from Leicester Square to Tower Hill. Follow the paving stones marked with jubilee crowns, or buy a booklet from the London Tourist Board.

Spitalfields is steeped in history and a fascinating area to explore. Get hold of the free *A Walk Through Spitalfields* from the London Tourist Board Offices and explore it for yourself.

Organised walks

Citisights of London uses professional archaeologists who have worked at the Museum of London as guides, and groups are taken on tours that last about two hours. Typical themes are Roman, Saxon and Medieval London, Chaucer and Whittington's London, and 2000 Years Around London Bridge. There's a charge, with reduced prices for students and children under the age of 8 going along free. Standard walks normally take place from the Museum of London Tuesday–Sunday at 14.30 and Thursday evenings at 19.30, but Citisights will also arrange special walks or complete days out for groups of 10 or more.

Clerkenwell Heritage/Urban Studies Centre organises walks through this little-known area of London. You'll be surprised at its hidden charms.

Discovering London offers a varied programme of walks, all with a theme. There's The Great Fire and Plague, Evil London – Crime Through the Ages, and London's Hidden Alleys and Courtyards, for instance. If you are accompanied by an adult and are under the age of 16, it's a free jaunt.

Inland Waterways Association organises guided walks along the Regent Canal during the summer and autumn.

London Walks have a varied programme. You can follow the dreadful route of Jack the Ripper, inspect the haunts of ghosts, discover Dickens' London, or join in at least a dozen more jaunts. All you have to do is turn up outside a designate tube station at the right time on the right day and you'll find a friendly guide waiting for you. Provided you are accompanied by an adult, if you're under 16 you can tag along for free. Walkabout tickets will save you money if you intend to go on more than two or three walks. London Walks, 139 Conway Road, N14 7BH, tel 882 2763

Ramblers' Association is an organisation with about a dozen enthusiastic local groups in London. Not a great many walks are arranged in London, but there's usually one to the country on Sundays. People usually join as a family unit, but if you're really keen, ring for further information.

Richmond Society Heritage Walks take place every other Wednesday May–September, starting from the entrance to Richmond station. Further information from Richmond Tourist Information Centres.

Streets of London offer twelve different tours of London, each illustrating a different aspect of London. There's no need to book. You just turn up at the time and place stated, and your guide will be there, but be prepared for a 1½–2 hour trip. If you are under 16 and accompanied by an adult, it's free. Walks include Haunted London, Shakespeare's London, Lawyers' London and The London of Sherlock Holmes.

Workshops

Workshops are places that offer a multiplicity of activities and cater for people of all ages. They usually function in the evenings, at weekends and during the school holidays.

Centres

Battersea Arts Centre has acrobatics, ballet, craft, dance, drama, guitar, gymnastics, puppetry and story sessions. It's open for families and pre-school children during the day and caters for those after school 15.00–17.00. There are Sunday sessions for parents and children, and in the holidays it offers cartoons, magicians and special events. (Refreshments.)

Camden Arts Centre has a number of classes for children at weekends. There are three age groups – 5–7, 7–11 and 12–16. Activities include collage, crafts, crochet, drama, embroidery, painting, paper and card construction, mask-making, printmaking and sculpture. There are special workshops during the school holidays.

Island Art Centre has a wide variety of courses and projects such as pottery, art, video, printing and crafts.

London Central YMCA has a junior programme after school, at weekends and during the school holidays. As well as varied sports activities, there are workshops in art and craft, chess, pottery, dance, drama and photography. If you are aged 11–16, you can buy an annual membership card and pay reduced entry instead of rather more for each visit.

Morley College Workshops are organised for the whole family on Saturdays, and there's a one-week summer workshop in the holidays. Neither children nor parents can use its facilities on their own – the emphasis is on family participation. Activities include music, art and crafts, astronomy, music-making, languages and family concerts.

Oval House is for those aged 16 and over. It has an exhilarating atmosphere and is alive with activity. You can become involved in music, become an expert in stilt dancing, tumbling or clowning, or take part in drama activities. Oval House possesses two theatres.

Maps

Map 1: Kew and Richmond

to Wembley

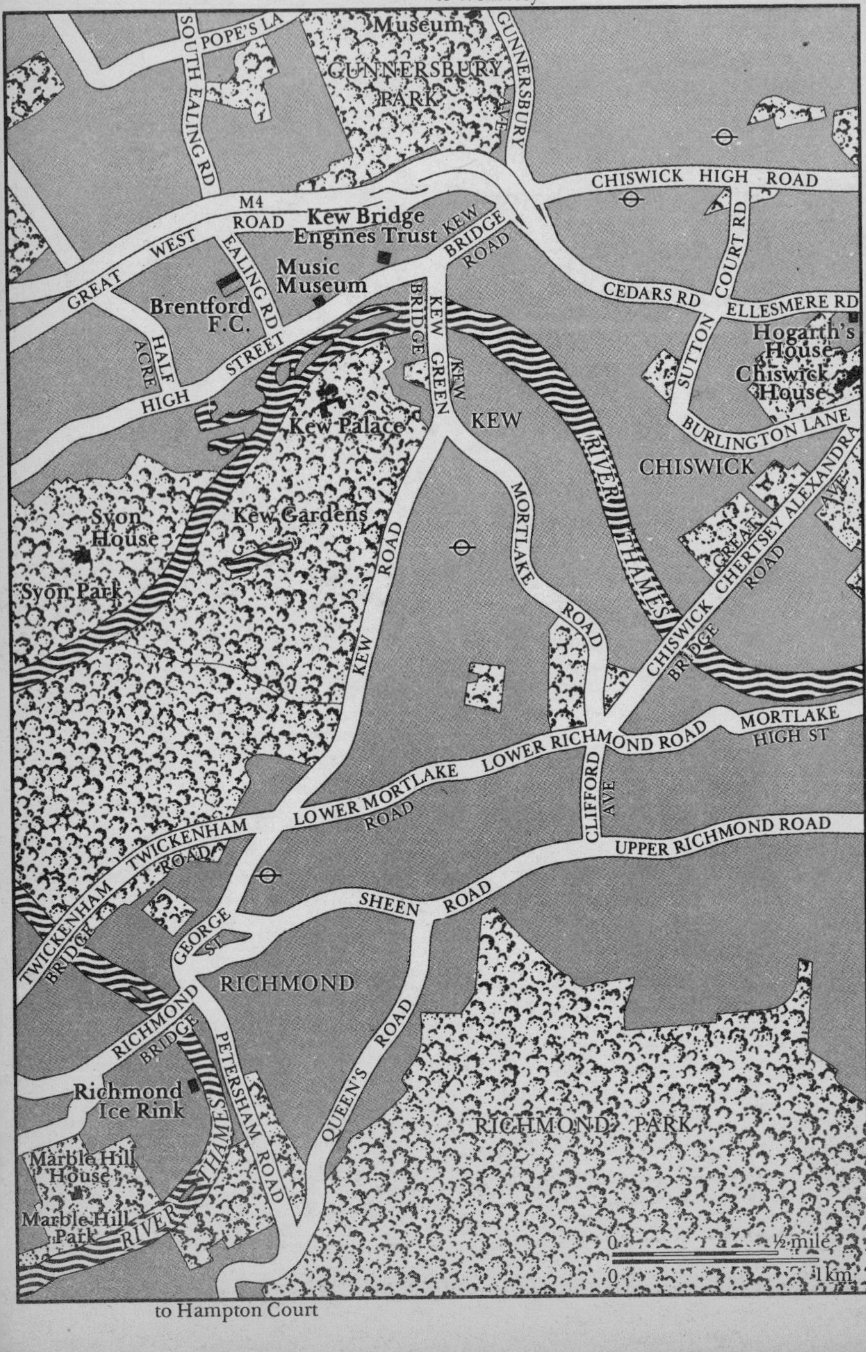

to Hampton Court

Museum

GUNNERSBURY PARK

SOUTH EALING RD

POPE'S LA

GUNNERSBURY

CHISWICK HIGH ROAD

M4 ROAD

Kew Bridge Engines Trust

KEW BRIDGE

WEST

GREAT

EALING RD

KEW BRIDGE ROAD

CEDARS RD

ELLESMERE RD

Music Museum

Brentford F.C.

HALF ACRE

STREET

HIGH

BRIDGE

KEW GREEN

KEW

SUTTON COURT RD

Hogarth's House

Chiswick House

Kew Palace

BURLINGTON LANE

CHISWICK

RIVER THAMES

Syon House

Kew Gardens

KEW ROAD

MORTLAKE ROAD

GREAT CHERTSEY ROAD

AVE

ALEXANDRA

Syon Park

CHISWICK BRIDGE

LOWER RICHMOND ROAD

MORTLAKE HIGH ST

LOWER MORTLAKE ROAD

CLIFFORD AVE

UPPER RICHMOND ROAD

TWICKENHAM ROAD

SHEEN ROAD

TWICKENHAM BRIDGE

GEORGE ST

QUEEN'S ROAD

RICHMOND

RICHMOND PARK

RICHMOND BRIDGE

PETERSHAM ROAD

Richmond Ice Rink

RIVER THAMES

Marble Hill House

Marble Hill Park

0   ½ mile

0   1 km

Map 2: Fulham and Kensington

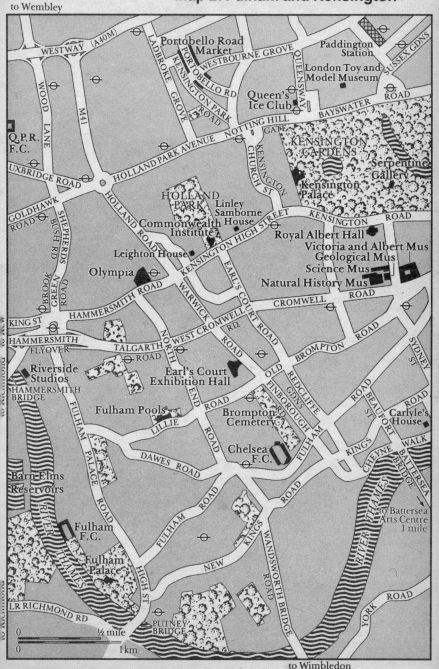

to Wembley

WESTWAY (A40M)

Portobello Road Market

WESTBOURNE GROVE

Paddington Station

London Toy and Model Museum

SUSSEX GDNS

Queen's Ice Club

BAYSWATER ROAD

WOOD LANE

M41

LADBROKE GROVE

PORTOBELLO RD

KENSINGTON PARK ROAD

QUEENSWAY

Q.P.R. F.C.

NOTTING HILL GATE

KENSINGTON GARDENS

Serpentine Gallery

UXBRIDGE ROAD

HOLLAND PARK AVENUE

KENSINGTON CHURCH ST

Kensington Palace

GOLDHAWK ROAD

HOLLAND ROAD

HOLLAND PARK

Linley Samborne House

Commonwealth Institute

KENSINGTON ROAD

Royal Albert Hall

KENSINGTON HIGH STREET

Victoria and Albert Mus
Geological Mus
Science Mus
Natural History Mus

SHEPHERDS BUSH RD

Leighton House

Olympia

HAMMERSMITH ROAD

WARWICK

EARL'S COURT ROAD

CROMWELL ROAD

GREEN ROAD

KING ST

HAMMERSMITH FLYOVER

TALGARTH ROAD

NORTH

WEST CROMWELL ROAD

RD.

OLD BROMPTON ROAD

BROMPTON ROAD

SYDNEY ST

Riverside Studios

HAMMERSMITH BRIDGE

Earl's Court Exhibition Hall

END ROAD

REDCLIFFE GDNS

FINBOROUGH ROAD

BEAUFORT ST

Carlyle's House

Fulham Pools

LILLIE

Brompton Cemetery

FULHAM ROAD

KINGS ROAD

CHEYNE WALK

BATTERSEA BRIDGE

Chelsea F.C.

DAWES ROAD

Barn Elms Reservoirs

FULHAM PALACE ROAD

RIVER THAMES

to Battersea Arts Centre 1 mile

Fulham F.C.

FULHAM ROAD

NEW KINGS ROAD

WANDSWORTH BRIDGE ROAD

RIVER THAMES

YORK ROAD

Fulham Palace

HIGH ST

LR RICHMOND RD

PUTNEY BRIDGE

0   ½ mile

0   1 km

to Wimbledon

Map 3: The West End

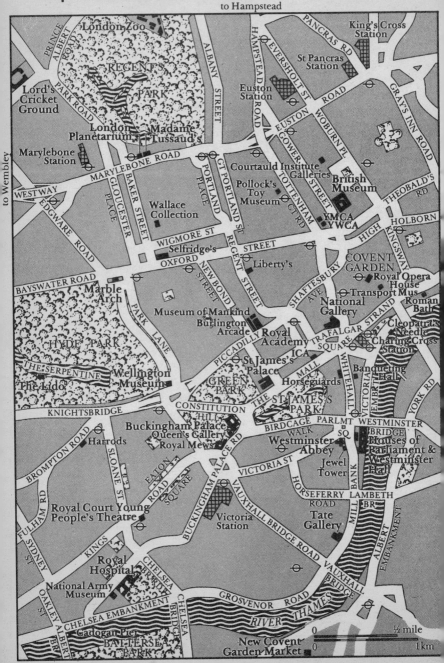

Map 4: The City and Southwark

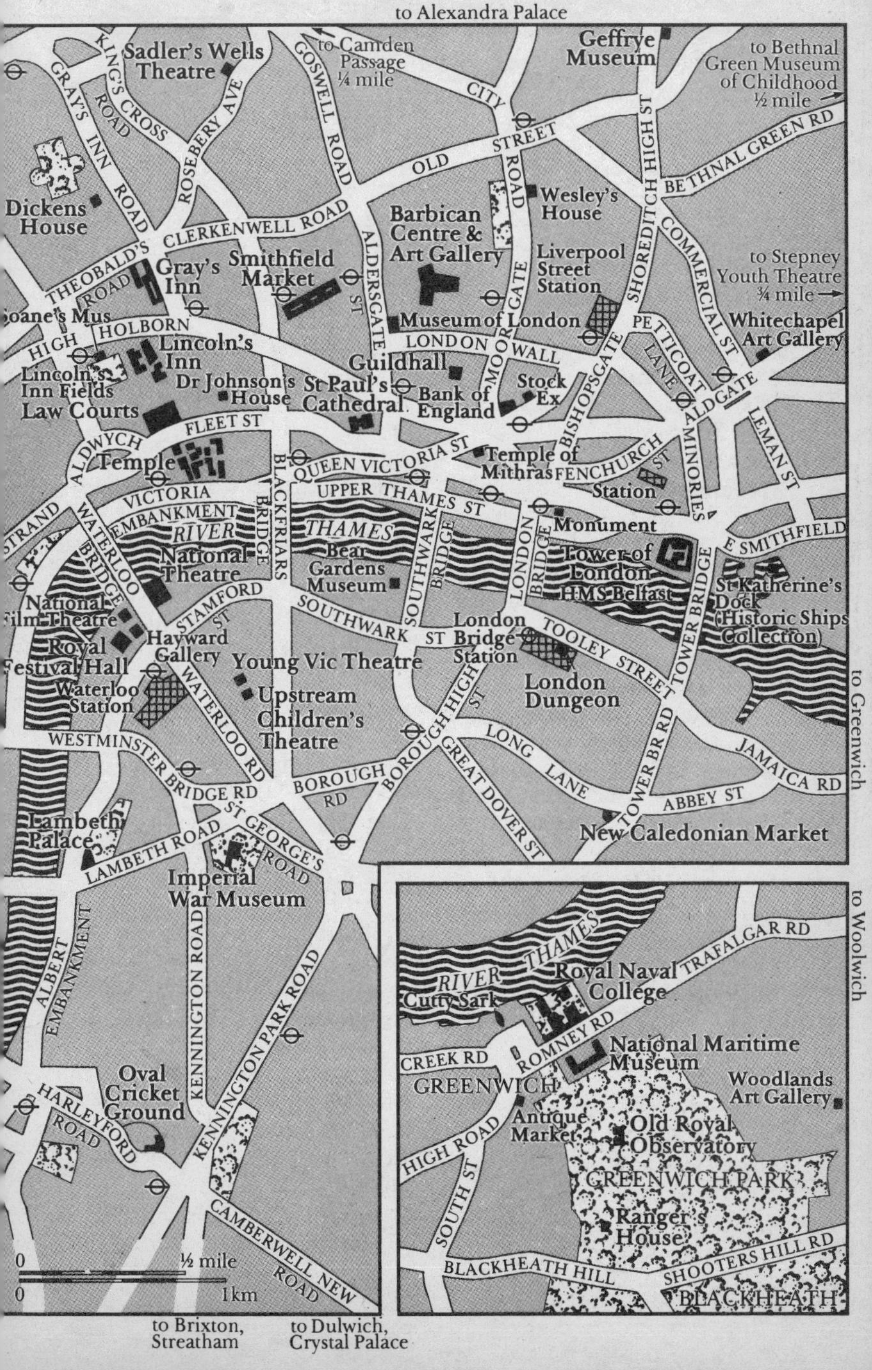

to Alexandra Palace

to Camden Passage ¼ mile

to Bethnal Green Museum of Childhood ½ mile

to Stepney Youth Theatre ¾ mile →

to Greenwich

to Woolwich

to Brixton, Streatham

to Dulwich, Crystal Palace

KING'S CROSS

GRAY'S INN ROAD

ROSEBERY AVE

GOSWELL ROAD

CITY

OLD STREET

ROAD

Sadler's Wells Theatre

Geffrye Museum

SHOREDITCH HIGH ST

BETHNAL GREEN RD

COMMERCIAL ST

Dickens House

CLERKENWELL ROAD

THEOBALD'S ROAD

Gray's Inn

Smithfield Market

ALDERSGATE ST

Barbican Centre & Art Gallery

Wesley's House

Liverpool Street Station

PETTICOAT LANE

Whitechapel Art Gallery

HIGH HOLBORN

Soane's Mus

Lincoln's Inn

Dr Johnson's House

Museum of London

LONDON WALL

MOORGATE

BISHOPSGATE

ALDGATE

LEMAN ST

Lincoln's Inn Fields

Law Courts

St Paul's Cathedral

Guildhall

Bank of England

Stock Ex

FENCHURCH ST

MINORIES

E SMITHFIELD

FLEET ST

Temple

ALDWYCH

STRAND

VICTORIA EMBANKMENT

WATERLOO BRIDGE

BLACKFRIARS BRIDGE

QUEEN VICTORIA ST

UPPER THAMES ST

Temple of Mithras

Fenchurch Station

RIVER THAMES

National Theatre

Bear Gardens Museum

SOUTHWARK BRIDGE

SOUTHWARK ST

Monument

LONDON BRIDGE

Tower of London

HMS Belfast

TOWER BRIDGE

St Katherine's Dock (Historic Ships Collection)

National Film Theatre

Royal Festival Hall

Hayward Gallery

STAMFORD ST

Young Vic Theatre

London Bridge Station

TOOLEY STREET

JAMAICA RD

Waterloo Station

WATERLOO RD

Upstream Children's Theatre

London Dungeon

WESTMINSTER BRIDGE RD

BOROUGH RD

BOROUGH HIGH ST

GREAT DOVER ST

LONG LANE

ABBEY ST

TOWER BR RD

Lambeth Palace

LAMBETH ROAD

ST GEORGE'S ROAD

Imperial War Museum

New Caledonian Market

ALBERT EMBANKMENT

KENNINGTON ROAD

KENNINGTON PARK ROAD

Oval Cricket Ground

HARLEYFORD ROAD

CAMBERWELL NEW ROAD

0 ½ mile

0 1km

Greenwich inset

to Greenwich

RIVER THAMES

Royal Naval College

TRAFALGAR RD

Cutty Sark

CREEK RD

ROMNEY RD

National Maritime Museum

Woodlands Art Gallery

GREENWICH

HIGH ROAD

SOUTH ST

Antique Market

Old Royal Observatory

GREENWICH PARK

Ranger's House

BLACKHEATH HILL

SHOOTERS HILL RD

BLACKHEATH

INDEX

Key:
XE = Christmas Eve
XD = Christmas day
BD = Boxing Day

PH = Public Holidays
NYD = New Year's Day
GF = Good Friday
MD = May Day

British Museum, Great Russell Street WC1, tel.636 1555. *Open:* Monday–Saturday 10.00–17.00, Sunday 14.30–18.30. *Closed:* NYD, GF, MD, XE, XD, BD. *Tube:* Goodge Street, Holborn, Russell Square, Tottenham Court Road. *Bus:* 5, 7, 8, 19, 22, 25, 38, 68, 77A, 155, 172, 188 to Southampton Row; 7, 8, 19, 22, 25, 38, 55 to New Oxford Street; 14, 24, 29, 73, 134, 176 to Great Russell Street. pp.29, 40, 42, 56, 69, 73, 77, 106, 112, 129, 151

British Waterways Board, Melbury House, Melbury Terrace NW1, tel.262 6711. *Tube/BR:* Marylebone. *Bus:* 1, 18, 27, 159, 176. p.114

Brixton Market (Electric Avenue, Pope's Road, Brixton Station Road) SW9. *Open:* Monday–Saturday (not Wednesday afternoon). *Tube:* Brixton. *Bus:* 2, 2B, 3, 35, 37, 45, 50, 95, 109, 133, 159, 172, 196, P4. p.132

Brixton Mill, Brixton Hill SW2, tel.674 6141. *Tube:* Brixton. *Bus:* 50, 95, 109, 133, 159. p.126

Brockwell Park SE24. *Tube:* Brixton, then bus 2, 2B, 3, 37, 172, 196; Clapham Common, then bus 37. *Bus:* 2, 2B, 3, 37, 40, 68, 172, 196. pp.20, 35, 101

Bromley-by-Bow Tidemill, Three Mills Lane E3. *Tube:* Bromley-by-Bow. *Bus:* 52, 108, 225. p.126

Brompton Cemetery, Brompton Road SW3. *Tube:* West Brompton. *Bus:* 11, 14, 22, 28, 30, 31, 74. p.106

Broomfield Museum, Broomfield Park N13, tel.882 1354. *Open:* Easter–September Tuesday–Friday 10.00–18.00, Saturday, Sunday 10.00–20.00 (until 17.00 October–Easter or park closing time if earlier). *Closed:* Monday (tel. for details of PH). *Tube:* Arnos Grove; Southgate. *BR:* Palmers Green. *Bus:* 29, 121, 123, 298, W9. pp.92, 140, 151

Broxbourne Lido, Old Nazeing Road, Broxbourne, Hertfordshire, tel.0992 442841. *Travel:* see Boat Centre. p.166

Bruce Castle Museum, Lordship Lane N17, tel.808 8772. *Open:* Tuesday–Friday 10.00–17.00, Saturday 10.00–12.30, 13.30–17.00. *Closed:* Monday (tel. for details of PH). *BR:* Bruce Grove. *Tube:* Seven Sisters; Wood Green then bus 243. *Bus:* 76, 123, 149, 171, 243, 243A, 259, 279, 279A. pp.42, 77, 165

Bubble Theatre Company, 9 Kingsford Street NW5, tel.485 3420. *Tube:* Belsize Park. *Bus:* 24, 46, C11. p.171

Buckingham Palace, The Mall SW1. *Tube:* Green Park, Hyde Park Corner, St James's Park, Victoria. *Bus:* 2, 2B, 9, 10, 11, 14, 16, 19, 22, 24, 25, 29, 30, 36, 36A, 36B, 38, 39, 52, 52A, 55, 70, 73, 74, 76, 137, 149, 185, 500, 507. pp.17, 25, 27, 116, 144

September Wednesday, Sunday 14.00–17.00 (Chelsea Flower week 12.00–17.00). *Travel:* see Royal Hospital. p.101

Chelsea Pottery, 13 Radnor Walk SW3, tel.352 1366. *Tube:* Sloane Square. *Bus:* 11, 19, 22. p.151

Chessington Zoo, Leatherhead Road, Chessington, Surrey, tel.78 27227. *Open:* summer daily 10.00–17.00; winter daily 10.00–16.00. *Closed:* XD. *BR:* Chessington South. *Bus:* 65, 71; 152 (Sundays only). *Green Line:* 714. *London Country:* 468. pp.37, 98

Children's Film Unit, 8 Ashridge House, Carlton Road, Sidcup, Kent, tel.302 0611. p.70

Chiswick House, Burlington Lane W4, tel.994 3299. *Open:* mid-March–mid-October daily 9.30–18.30; mid-October–mid-March Wednesday–Sunday 9.30–16.30. *Closed:* mid-October–mid-March Monday–Tuesday, NYD, XE, XD, BD. *Tube:* Hammersmith, then bus 290. *Bus:* 290, E3. pp.120, 160

Church Farm House Museum, Greyhound Hill NW4, tel.203 0130. *Open:* Monday,

Wednesday–Saturday 10.00–13.00, 14.00–17.30, Tuesday 10.00–13.00, Sunday 14.00–17.30. *Closed:* XE, XD, BD (tel. for details of PH). *Tube:* Hendon Central. *Bus:* 113. p.160

Citisights of London, 12 Alpha Place SW3, tel.600 3699, ext. 281. p.177

City of London Information Centre, St Paul's Churchyard EC4, tel.606 3030. *Open:* April–September Monday–Friday 9.30–17.00, Saturday 10.00–16.00; October–March Monday–Friday 9.30–17.00, Saturday 10.00–12.30. *Travel:* see St Paul's Cathedral. p.128

Clapham Common, SW4. *Tube:* Clapham Common, Clapham South. *Bus:* 37, 88, 118, 155, 181, 181A, 189. pp.21, 99

Cleopatra's Needle, Victoria Embankment WC2. *Tube:* Embankment. *Bus:* 109, 155, 168, 172, 184. p.142

Clerkenwell Green Association of Craftsmen, Pennybank Chambers, Clerkenwell Road EC1, tel.250 1039 (for information). *Tube:* Farringdon. *Bus:* 19, 38, 63, 168A, 171, 172, 221, 259. p.44

Clerkenwell Heritage/Urban Studies Centre, 33 St John's Square EC1, tel.250 1039. p.128, 177
See above Clerkenwell Road

Clink Street, Southwark SE1. *Tube:* London Bridge. *Bus:* 8A, 10, 18, 21, 35, 40, 40A, 43, 44, 47, 48, 70, 95, 133, 501, 513. p.142

Clissold Park N16. *Tube:* Finsbury Park, Manor House. *Bus:* 73, 106, 141, 171. p.35

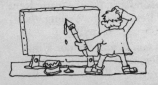

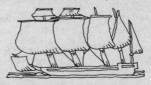

223, 285, A1, A2. pp.112, 176

Henry VIII's Wine Cellar,
Whitehall SW1. *Open:* March–
September Saturday afternoon.
Travel: see Banqueting Hall. p.121

Highgate Cemetery, Swains Lane,
N6. *Tube:* Archway. *Bus:* 143, 210,
239, 271, C11.

HMS *Belfast*, Symon's Wharf,
Vine Lane, Tooley Street SE1,
tel.407 6434. *Open:* summer daily
11.00–17.50, winter daily
11.00–16.30. *Closed:* NYD, GF,
MD, XE, XD, BD. *Tube:* London
Bridge, Tower Hill. *Bus:* 8A, 10,
18, 35, 40, 42, 43, 44, 47, 48, 70,
78, 133, 188, 501, 503. *Ferry:* see
Boats (Boat Trips). p.54

Herne Hill Stadium, off Half
Moon Lane SE24. *BR:* North
Dulwich, Herne Hill. *Bus:* 2, 3, 40,
68, 172, 196, P4. p.86

Hillingdon Youth Sports Centre,
Judge Heath Lane, Hayes,
Middlesex, tel.573 3431. *BR:*
Hayes and Harlington. *Bus:* 204.
pp.51, 162, 167

Historic Ships Collection, East
Basin, St Katherine's Dock E1,
tel.481 0043. *Open:* daily
10.00–17.00 (until 19.00 July–
August). *Closed:* NYD, XD. *Tube:*
Tower Hill. *Bus:* 23, 42, 78. p.55

Hogarth's House, Hogarth Lane,
Chiswick W4, tel.994 6757. *Open:*
Monday–Saturday 11.00–18.00,
Sunday 14.00–18.00 (until 16.00
in winter). *Closed:* Tuesday; 1st
two weeks in September, last three
weeks in December. *Tube:*

Hammersmith, then bus 290. *Bus:*
290. pp.95, 112

Holland Park, Kensington W14,
tel. 602 2226. *Tube:* Holland Park,
High Street Kensington, Earls
Court. *Bus:* 9, 12, 27, 28, 31, 33,
49, 73, 88. pp.31, 35, 36, 46, 48,
101, 147

Holy Sepulchre, Holborn
Viaduct EC1, tel.248 1660. *Tube:*
Chancery Lane. *Bus:* 8, 18, 22, 25,
45, 46, 63, 171, 221, 243, 259.
pp.22, 25, 138

Horham School, Charlwood Road
SW15, tel.788 2157. *BR:* Putney.
Tube: Putney Bridge. *Bus:* 14, 22,
30, 37, 39, 74, 85, 93, 220, 264.
p.151

Horniman Gardens, tel.699 8924,
see Horniman Museum. pp.31, 36,
46

Horniman Museum, Forest Hill
SE23, tel.699 2339 (nature trail,
tel.699 8924). *Open:* Monday–
Saturday 10.30–18.00, Sunday
14.00–18.00. *Closed:* XE, XD (tel.
for information about BD). *BR:*
Forest Hill. *Bus:* 12, 12A, 63, 122,
124, 124A, 171, 176, 185, 194, P4.
pp.29, 44, 73, 92, 99, 106, 112,
139, 140, 151

Horse Guards, Whitehall SW1.
Travel: see Banqueting Hall.
pp.17, 18, 20, 27

House of St Barnabus, 1 Greek
Street W1, tel.437 1894. *Open:*
Wednesday 14.30–16.15,
Thursday 11.00–12.30 or by
appointment. *Travel:* see Berwick
Street Market. p.121

Houses of Parliament,
Parliament Square SW1, tel.219
3000. *Open:* (when Parliament is in
recess): Saturday, Easter and
Spring BH Mondays; August
Tuesday, Thursday; September

Thursday. *Entrance:* public
entrance in Victoria Tower
10.00–16.30. *Open:* (when
Parliament is sitting): to
Strangers' Gallery in either house
by advance application to a peer
or MP or by queueing at St
Stephen's entrance (queue
admitted to House of Lords
Monday to Wednesday from
about 14.30, Thursday at 15.00;
queue admitted to House of
Commons Monday–Thursday
16.30, occasionally Friday at about
11.00). *Note:* queue moves very
slowly. *Travel:* see Westminster
Abbey. pp.25, 112, 121

Hyde Park W1. *Tube:* Marble
Arch, Hyde Park Corner,
Knightsbridge, Lancaster Gate.
Bus: 2, 2B, 6, 7, 8, 9, 12, 14, 15, 16,
16A, 19, 22, 23, 25, 30, 36, 36B,
38, 52, 52A, 55, 73, 74, 88, 137,
500.
pp.15, 148

IBA Broadcasting Gallery, 70
Brompton Road SW3, tel.584
7011. *Tube:* Knightsbridge. *Bus:*
14, 30, 74. pp.112, 156

ICA Children's Cinema Club *see*
Institute of Contemporary Arts.
p.69

Imber Court, East Molesey,

tel.398 1109. *BR:* East Molesey.
p.20

Imperial Collection, Central Hall
SW1, tel.222 0770. *Open:*
Monday–Saturday 10.00–18.00.
Closed: Sunday (tel. for details of
PH). *Travel:* see Westminster
Abbey. pp.112, 129

Imperial War Museum, Lambeth
Road SE1, tel.735 8922. *Open:*
Monday–Saturday 10.00–18.00,
Sunday 14.00–18.00. *Closed:*
NYD, GF, MD, XE, XD, BD. *Tube:*
Lambeth North, Elephant and
Castle. *Bus:* 1, 3, 10, 12, 44, 45, 53,
63, 68, 109 Saturday only), 141,
155 (Monday–Friday), 159, 171,
172 (not Sunday), 176 (Monday–
Friday), 177, 188. pp.33, 42, 46,
66, 69, 77, 112, 135

Inland Waterways Association,
114 Regent's Park Road, NW1.
Travel: see English Folk Song and
Dance Society. p.178

Institute of Contemporary Arts,
Nash House, The Mall SW1,
tel.930 3647. *Travel:* see
Banqueting Hall, Buckingham
Palace. p.69

Inter-Action Trust Ltd, Talacre
Open Space, 15 Wilkin Street
NW5, tel.485 0881. *Tube:* Kentish
Town. *Bus:* 3, 24, 27, 46, 134, 137,
214. pp.78, 171

Intimate Theatre, Green Lanes,
Palmers Green N13, tel.886 5451.
Tube: Southgate. *Bus:* 29, 123,
125. p.171

Inverness Street Market, Camden
Town NW1. *Open:* Wednesday,
Friday, Saturday. *Tube:* Camden
Town. *Bus:* 3, 24, 27, 29, 31, 46,
56, 68, 74, 134, 137, 214, 253.
p.133

Island Art Centre, Tiller Road
Baths E14, tel.987 7925. *BR:*

182, 186, 258, 286. pp.113, 149

Lambeth Palace, Lambeth Palace Road SE1, tel.928 6222. *Tube:* Westminster, then bus 3, 77, 159, 170. *Bus:* 3, 10, 44, 77, 149, 159, 170, 307. p.145

Last Chance Centre, 87 Masbro Road W14, tel.603 7118. *Tube:* Hammersmith, Olympia, Shepherd's Bush. *Bus:* 9, 27, 28, 33, 73 to Olympia; 12, 49, 88, 105, 207, 220, 237, 283, 295 to Shepherd's Bush, 72. pp.79, 151

Lauderdale House, Waterlow Park N6, tel.348 8717. *Tube:* Archway. *Bus:* 143, 210, 271. pp.169, 171

Law Courts *see* Royal Courts of Justice.

Lawn Tennis Association, Queens Club, Palliser Road W14, tel.385 4233. p.167

Leadenhall Market, Gracechurch Street EC3. *Open:* Monday–Friday. *Tube:* Bank, Monument. *Bus:* 10, 15, 25, 40, 35, 48, 47, 44, 8A. p.133

Leaside Youth Centre, Springfield Road E15, tel.806 6887. *BR:* West Ham. *Bus:* 69, 173, 241. pp.64, 117

Leather Lane, Holborn EC1. *Open:* Monday–Saturday. *Tube:* Chancery Lane, Farringdon. *Bus:* 5, 8, 18, 19, 22, 25, 38, 45, 46, 55, 63, 171, 172, 243, 259, 501. p.133

Lee Valley Ice Centre, Lea Bridge Road, Leyton E10, tel.533

3151. *BR:* Lea Bridge, Clapton, then bus 38, 48, 55. *Bus:* 38, 48, 55, 255. p.125

Lee Valley Park, Enfield, Middlesex, tel.Lea Valley 717711. *BR:* Waltham Cross, Cheshunt, Broxbourne. *Bus:* Leisurebus (circular route round park connecting stations). pp.36, 54, 148, 155

Lee Valley Viaduct Market, Edmonton E4. *Open:* Sunday morning. *BR:* Angel Road. *Bus:* 34, 102, 144. p.134

Leighton House, 12 Holland Park Road W14, tel.602 3316. *Open:* Monday–Saturday 11.00–17.00 (until 18.00 Monday–Friday during temporary exhibitions). *Tube:* High Street Kensington. *Bus:* 9, 27, 28, 31, 33, 49, 73. p.46

Leytonstone Recreation Centre, Cathall Road E11, tel.539 8343. *BR:* Leytonstone High Road. *Tube:* Leyton. *Bus:* 10, 58, 69, 158, 262. p.163

Liberty & Co. Ltd, Regent Street W1, tel.734 1234. *Tube:* Oxford Circus. *Bus:* 1, 3, 6, 7, 8, 12, 13, 15, 16A, 23, 25, 53, 73, 88, 137, 159, 500. p.75

Light Fantastic Gallery of Holography, 48 South Road, Covent Garden WC2, tel.836 6423. *Open:* Monday–Saturday 10.00–20.00, Sunday 12.00–18.00. *Closed:* ring for details. *Travel:* see London Transport Museum. p.156

London Planetarium,
Marylebone Road NW1, tel.486
1121. *Open:* daily 11.00–16.30 (tel.
for details of performances).
Closed: XD. *Tube:* Baker Street.
Bus: 1, 2, 2B, 13, 18, 27, 30, 74,
113, 159, 176. pp.49, 156

London Stone *see* Bank of China.
p.39

London Toy and Model Museum,
October House, 23 Craven Hill
W2, tel.262 7905. *Open:* Tuesday–
Saturday 10.00–17.30, Sunday,
BH Mondays 11.00–17.00. *Closed:*
Monday (not BH; tel. for details
of PH). *Tube:* Paddington,
Bayswater, Lancaster Gate,
Queensway. *Bus:* 12, 88. pp.92,
113, 134

London Transport Museum,
Wellington Street, Covent Garden
WC2E 7BB, tel.379 6344. *Open:*
daily 10.00–18.00. *Closed:* XD,
BD. *Tube:* Covent Garden,
Leicester Square. *Bus:* 1, 6, 9, 11,
13, 15, 24, 29, 77, 77A, 88, 159,
170, 172, 176. pp.66, 113, 116,
135

London Walks, 139 Conway Road
N14, tel.882 2763. *BR:* Palmers
Green. *Bus:* 298, 121. p.178

London Zoo, Regent's Park NW1,
tel.722 3333. *Open:* March–
October 9.00–18.00, Sundays,

Bank Holidays 9.00–19.00;
November–February 10.00–18.00
or dusk. *Closed:* XD. *Tube:* Baker
Street; Camden Town, then bus
74. *Bus:* 2, 3, 53, 74. *Boat:* see
Boats. pp.37, 113

Lord's Cricket Ground, St John's
Wood NW1, tel.289 1616. *Tube:* St
John's Wood. *Bus:* 2, 2B, 8, 13, 46,
74, 74B, 113, 159. p.83

**Lordship Lane Recreation
Ground**, Walpole Road N17,
tel.808 0639. *BR:* Bruce Grove.
Tube: Turnpike Lane. *Bus:* 123,
144, 144A, 231, 217. p.86

Lyric Theatre, King Street,
Hammersmith W6, tel.741 2311.
Tube: Hammersmith. *Bus:* 27, 91,
237, 267, 290. p.171

Madame Tussaud's, Marylebone
Road NW1. *Open:* April–
September daily 10.00–18.00
(until 17.30 October–March).
Closed: XD. *Travel:* see London
Planetarium. pp.93, 107, 113

Mall SW1. *Travel:* see Trafalgar
Square, Buckingham Palace.
pp.17, 20, 158

Mansion House, Mansion House
Street EC4, tel.626 2500. *Tube:*
Mansion House. *Bus:* 8, 9, 11, 15,
21, 25, 43, 76, 133, 501. p.22

Marble Arch W1. *Tube:* Marble Arch. *Bus:* 2, 2B, 6, 7, 8, 12, 15, 16, 16A, 23, 25, 30, 36, 36A, 36B, 73, 74, 88, 137, 500. p.142

Marble Hill House and Park, Richmond Road, Twickenham, Middlesex, tel.892 5115. *Open:* February–October Saturday–Thursday 10.00–17.00 (until 16.00 November–January). *Closed:* XE, XD. *Tube:* Richmond. *Bus:* 27, 33, 37, 90B, 202, 270, 290. p.31, 113, 121

Marble Hill Park, tel.892 1900. *Travel:* see Marble Hill House. p.31

Marlborough House, Pall Mall SW1, tel.930 9249. *Tube:* Green Park. *Bus:* 9, 14, 19, 22, 25, 38, 55, to St James's Street. p.121

Martinware Pottery Collection, Public Library, 9–11 Osterley Park Road, Southall, Middlesex, tel.574 4312. *Open:* Monday 9.00–20.00, Tuesday 9.00–19.00, Thursday, Friday 9.00–17.00. *Closed:* Wednesday, XE, PH. *BR:* Southall. *Bus:* 105, 195, 232. p.151

Maryon-Wilson Park SE7. *BR:* Charlton, then bus 177, 180. *Bus:* 177, 180. p.36

Michael Sobell Sports Centre, Hornsey Road N7, tel.607 1632. *Tube:* Finsbury Park. *Bus:* 14, 19, 29, 221, 253, 259, 279, 279A. pp.64, 117, 125, 155, 159, 163

Mile End Park, Clemence Street E14, tel.980 1885. *Tube:* Mile End. *Bus:* 5, 10, 15, 23, 25, 40, 56, 106, 277. p.31

Molecule Theatre, Mermaid Theatre, Puddle Dock EC4, tel.236 9521, ext. 259. *Travel:* see Mansion House. p.156

Monument, nr Monument Street EC4, tel.626 6881. *Open:* April–September Monday–Friday 9.00–17.40, Sunday 14.00–17.40 (until 16.00 October–March). *Closed:* Saturday, NYD, XD, BD. *Tube:* Monument. *Bus:* 8A, 10, 21, 23, 35, 40, 43, 44, 47, 48, 133, 501, 513. pp.97, 176

Moonshine Community Arts Workshop, Victor Road NW10, tel.969 7959. p.79

Morley College, Westminster Bridge Road SE1, tel.928 8501. *Tube:* Lambeth North. *Bus:* 12, 53, 109, 149, 155, 159, 170, 171, 172, 184. pp.136, 137, 179

Mornington Sports and Leisure Centre, Underhill Passage, 142–50 Arlington Road NW1, tel.267 3600. *Tube:* Camden Town. *Bus:* 3, 24, 27, 29, 31, 53, 68, 74, 134, 137, 214, 253. p.163

Mountview Youth Theatre, 104 Crouch Hill N8, tel.340 5885. *BR:* Crouch Hill. *Bus:* W2, W7. p.170

Museum of Artillery, The Rotunda, Repository Road SE18, tel.856 5533, ext. 385. *Open:* April–October Monday–Friday 10.00–12.45, 14.00–17.00, Saturday 10.00–12.00, 14.00–17.00, Sunday 14.00–17.00 (until 16.00 November–March). *Closed:* NYD, GF, XD, BD. *BR:* Woolwich Arsenal. *Bus:* 53, 54, 75, 122A. pp.33, 42

Museum of Garden History, St Mary-at-Lambeth, Lambeth Palace Road SE1, tel.373 4030. *Open:* April–November Monday–Friday 11.00–15.00, Sunday

Wimbledon. *Bus:* 57, 80, 93, 131, 155. pp.113, 153, 170, 171

Pollock's Toy Museum, 1 Scala Street W1, tel.636 3452. *Open:* Monday–Saturday 10.00–17.00. *Closed:* Sunday, PH. *Tube:* Goodge Street. *Bus:* 14, 24, 29, 73, 134, 176. p.92

Porta Bella Packet, Ladbroke Grove/Kensal Road W10, tel.960 5456. *Tube:* Ladbroke Grove. *Bus:* 15, 295. pp.53, 113

Portobello Road Market, Notting Hill W11. *Open:* Monday–Saturday (not Thursday afternoon). *Tube:* Ladbroke Grove, Westbourne Park. *Bus:* 7, 15, 23, 28, 31, 52, 52A. p.134

Postman's Park *see* St Botolph's Without. p.143

Prince Henry's Room, 17 Fleet Street EC4, tel.363 7323. *Open:* Monday–Friday 13.45–17.00, Saturday 13.45–16.30. *Tube:* Temple. *Bus:* 4, 6, 9, 9A, 11, 15, 171, 502, 513. p.122

Public Records Office, Chancery Lane WC2, tel.405 3488. *Open:* Monday–Friday 13.00–16.00. *Closed:* PH. *Tube:* Chancery Lane, Temple. *Bus:* 4, 6, 9, 11, 15, 23, 77, 171, 502, 513. p.57

Pudding Lane EC3. *Travel:* see Monument. p.97

Puppet Theatre Barge, Camden Lock, Market Wharf NW1, tel.249 6876. *Travel:* see Camden Lock Market. p.153

Purcell Room *see* Royal Festival Hall. p.137

Queen Anne's Gate SW1. *Tube:* St James's Park. *Bus:* 11; 24, 29, 76. p.122

Queen Elizabeth Hall, South Bank SE1, tel.928 3191. *Travel:* see Hayward Gallery. p.137

Queen Elizabeth's Hunting Lodge, *see* Epping Forest Museum. p.40

Queen's Chapel of the Savoy, Savoy Hill, Strand WC2. *Open:* Tuesday–Friday (middle of the day only; closed in August). *Tube:* Embankment, Temple; *Bus:* 1, 4, 6, 9, 11, 13, 15, 23, 68, 77, 77A, 170, 171, 172, 176, 188, 501, 502, 513. p.122

Queen's Gallery, Buckingham Palace SW1. *Open:* Tuesday–Saturday 11.00–17.00, Sunday 14.00–17.00. *Travel:* see Buckingham Palace. pp.47, 113

Queen's Ice Club, Queensway W2, tel.229 0172. *Tube:* Bayswater, Queensway. *Bus:* 12, 88. p.125

Queen Mother Reservoir, Horton Road, Horton, Slough. *Bus:* 81. p.117

Questors Theatre, Mattock Lane, Ealing W5, tel.567 0011. *BR:* West Ealing. *Tube:* Ealing Broadway. *Bus:* 65, 83, 207, 274, E1, E2. p.170

Ramblers' Association, 1–5 Wandsworth Road SW8, tel.582 6826. *BR/Tube:* Vauxhall. *Bus:* 2, 2B, 36, 36A, 36B, 44, 77, 77A, 83, 170, 185. p.178

Ranger's House, Chesterfield Walk SE10, tel.853 0035. *Open:* daily 10.00–17.00 (until 16.00 November–January). *Closed:* GF, XE, XD. *BR:* Greenwich, Blackheath. *Bus:* 53, 54, 75, 89, 108B, 192 to Blackheath, 117, 180, 188 to Greenwich. pp.47, 113

Road; 45, 63, 109, 141, 155 to Blackfriars Road. pp.70, 172

Vale Farm Sports Centre, Watford Road, Wembley, Middlesex, tel.908 2528. *BR:* Sudbury + Harrow Road, North Wembley. *Bus:* 182, 245. p.164

Verulamium Museum, St Michael's Street, St Albans, Hertfordshire. *Open:* Summer Monday–Saturday 10.00–17.30, Sunday 14.00–17.30 (until 16.00 in winter). *Closed:* XE, XD, BD. *BR:* St Albans City. *Tube:* New Barnet, then bus 84 (London Country) to St Albans. *Green Line:* 707, 717, 724, 727 to St Albans. *London Country:* 340. pp.41, 77

Vestry House Museum, Vestry Road E17, tel.527 5544, ext. 4391. *Open:* Monday–Friday 10.00–17.30, Saturday 10.00–17.00. *Closed:* PH. *BR:* Walthamstow Centre. *Tube:* Walthamstow Central. *Bus:* 20, 34, 69, 97, 206, 212, 255, 262, 275. p.127

Victoria and Albert Museum, Cromwell Road SW7, tel.589 6371. *Open:* Monday–Thursday, Saturday 10.00–17.50, Sunday 14.30–17.50. *Closed:* Friday, NYD, MD, XE, XD, BD. *Travel:* see Geological Museum. pp.30, 43, 45, 47, 74, 83, 114, 130, 139, 141, 152

Victoria Embankment Gardens WC2. *Tube:* Embankment, Temple. *Bus:* 1, 6, 9, 11, 13, 15, 23, 77, 109, 155, 170, 172, 176, 184 to Victoria Embankment; 77A, 171, 68 to Strand. pp.48, 138

Victoria Park, Hackney E9, tel.985 1957 (Lido, tel.985 6774; athletics track, tel. 985 8065). *Tube:* Mile End. *BR:* Cambridge Heath. *Bus:* 8, 8A, 52, 106, 277. pp.31, 167

Vintners' Hall, Upper Thames Street EC4, tel.236 1863. *Travel:* see St Paul's Cathedral. pp.19, 143

Wallace Collection, Hertford House, Manchester Square W1, tel.935 0687. *Open:* Monday–Saturday 10.00–17.00, Sunday 14.00–17.00. *Closed:* NYD, GF, MD, XE, XD, BD. *Tube:* Bond Street, Marble Arch. *Bus:* 2, 2B, 6, 7, 8, 12, 15, 16, 16A, 23, 25, 30, 36, 36B, 73, 74, 88, 137 to Marble Arch; 1, 113, 159 to Bond Street. pp.43, 48, 74, 114, 152

Walnuts Sports Centre, Lych Gate Road, Orpington, Kent, tel.Orpington 70533. *BR:* Orpington. *Bus:* 51, 61, 208, 229, 261, 299. p.164

Waltham Abbey, Waltham Abbey, Essex. *BR:* Waltham Cross. *Bus:* 250A, 217B, 242, 250. p.90

Walthamstow High Street Market E17. *Open:* Thursday–Saturday. *Tube:* Walthamstow Central. *Bus:* 48, 69, 97, 206, 212, 255, 262, 275. p.134

Walthamstow Reservoirs, Ferry Lane N17, tel.808 1527. *Open:* 6.30–30 minutes before sunset. *Tube:* Tottenham Hale, Blackhorse Road. *Bus:* 41, 123, 230. pp.99, 117

Wanstead Flats E11, E12. *Tube:* Wanstead, then bus 101, 162. *Bus:*